on track ...
Creedence Clearwater Revival

every album, every song

Tony Thompson

SONIC**BOND**

sonicbondpublishing.com

Sonicbond Publishing Limited
www.sonicbondpublishing.co.uk
Email: info@sonicbondpublishing.co.uk

First Published in the United Kingdom 2022
First Published in the United States 2022

British Library Cataloguing in Publication Data:
A Catalogue record for this book is available from the British Library

ISBN 978-1-78952-237-2

Typeset in ITC Garamond & ITC Avant Garde
Printed and bound in England

Graphic design and typesetting: Full Moon Media

To Cassandra, my partner and inspiration: this is dedicated to you.

Thanks

I wasn't old enough to be a Creedence fan at the time but I can remember hearing 'Sweet Hitch-Hiker' on the car radio when I was about six. I can also recall early '70s television advertisements for a greatest hits album that sounded pretty good. Like more than a few of my Gen X contemporaries, I went nuts over the music of the 1960s in about 1980 when I was supposed to be listening to 'new wave.' A beat-up copy of *Pendulum* from an op shop introduced me to their music properly. A few years later, I was playing bass in a high school rockabilly band and suggested a cover of 'Hey Tonight'. The guitarist and I were starting to make a lot of connections between 1950s rock and roll, 'classic' rock and the music of our own time. Rockabilly was bubbling under some of the 'roots rock' music we were hearing in the mid-1980s. Bruce Springsteen's forays into the genre caught our attention and we noticed that the Boss sometimes covered Creedence songs like 'Travelin Band' in concert. Wait a minute! Creedence is a rockabilly band!

So, a thank you to that guitarist, Mike, who remains a close friend. We've been talking about rock and roll for almost 40 years and there is so much left to cover! Thanks to Stephen at Sonicbond for agreeing so quickly to a book about this band. I love reading the On Track titles and it has been a great experience writing two of them. My son, Henry, is a musician and he spent a lot of time listening to and discussing the musical elements in Creedence songs with me. I am very proud of him and glad that in addition to being father and son, we are also friends.

on track ...
Creedence Clearwater Revival

Contents

It was no accident that my interest in Creedence progressed from warm to obsessive at a time when I was in a state of emotional upheaval brought on by politics, drugs, writing blocks, and problematic personal relationships. It was also a time when I was feeling alienated from my favourite rock band, The Rolling Stones, partly because of Altamont, partly because of feminism, but mostly because I was tired of chasing Mick Jagger's mysterious soul through the mazes of fun house mirrors he had built to protect it. Maybe it was all the politics and all the drugs, but I craved a simpler, more direct, more human connection to rock and I connected with John Fogerty in a way I never could with Jagger.

Ellen Willis, from *Rolling Stone Illustrated History of Rock and Roll*, 1980.

The Early Years

Portola Junior High in El Cerrito, CA, was torn down about ten years ago. It had stood for over 60 years on the side of a hill which provided, according to an alumni social media page, great views. Unfortunately, hills, earthquakes, and junior highs are a bad combination and, in 2012, the students were moved to a temporary building on the site before the school reopened as Fred T Korematsu Middle School a few blocks west. The social media site continues to be a place for lively discussions of beloved teachers and long-ago home economics classes. It would be utterly unexceptional but for three students who attended in the late 1950s.

They met in various classes and found themselves, like kids before and since, hanging around the music room at lunchtime, picking up instruments and dreaming of rock and roll stardom. At first, it was John Fogerty on guitar and Doug Clifford on drums. The repertoire was what John could play at the time. 'Rumble' by Link Wray, Duane Eddy's 'Rebel Rouser', and, likely, 'Ranchy' by Bill Justis, the song that George Harrison had played for John Lennon on a Liverpool bus a year earlier. Soon, another Portola student, Stu Cook, joined on piano. They called themselves The Blue Velvets and they played their first gig sometime in September of 1959. It was a 'sock hop' at school and the band played a short set of instrumentals while their classmates danced. Ten years later, the same lineup, along with John's older brother Tom, would play to half a million people at Yasgur's Farm in upstate New York.

The following spring, the band recorded some demos backing Tom Fogerty. The acetates, if they are around, remain in the hands of the various members and have never been released. The band, by this point, had been taken under the wing of the El Cerrito Boys Club and found themselves playing gigs all over San Francisco in the summer of 1960 as representatives of the organisation. At one such gig, they met James Powell, a young R&B singer. He was impressed with the band and asked them to back him on a song he was planning to record. The band's first single was a year away, so it is difficult to know what The Blue Velvets sounded like at this point, but Powell heard something he liked. The details are fuzzy. John Fogerty remembers the session taking place at Coast Recorders, where Creedence would record their first album. John played bass and presumably, Stu is on piano with Doug on drums. It appeared on a small Los Gatos label called Christy Records and was reissued the following year. Powell had a good voice and the band sounds solid, but other than the fact that it is their first commercial recording, it is not particularly revelatory.

Tom Fogerty, John's older brother, had been singing in local bands and occasionally fronting The Blue Velvets. In 1961, he signed a recording contract with a new San Francisco label called Orchestra Records. They became Tommy Fogerty and The Blue Velvets. They recorded three singles. The first two are available on the 2001 Creedence box set or YouTube. They occasionally turn up for sale.

'C'mon Baby'/'Oh My Love' (Orchestra Records 6177)

Both songs are written by Tommy Fogerty. The A-side is a Richie Valens-style rockabilly number notable for John's fiery, albeit brief, guitar solo. It's basic stuff but if you listen carefully, you can hear one of Doug's signature rolls and something of the chemistry forming. 'Oh My Love' is a classic '50s-style ballad. Tom sings on both songs. His voice is higher than his brother's and he sounds like Bobby Freeman here.

'Have You Ever Been Lonely?'/'Bonita' (Orchestra Records 611010)

This one appeared later in 1961 (early 1962 by some accounts) and the A-side managed to get some local airplay. 'Have You Ever Been Lonely?' was written by 'Johnny' Fogerty. It's a mid-tempo 1950s-style ballad along the lines of Roy Orbison's 'Only The Lonely', which had been a hit the previous year. It's better produced and the band sounds tighter. 'Bonita', a Tom and John co-write is another Valens-style song that rocks harder than anything thus far. Listen to the guitar solo at the end and you can discern something of the Creedence sound emerging.

'Now You're Not Mine'/'Yes You Did' (Orchestra Records 6252201)

This one is mysteriously credited to Tommy Fogerty and the Blue Violets on the label and was their final single for Orchestra. The A-side is another John Fogerty original that sounds like Frankie Avalon's 'Gingerbread' and other up-tempo pop songs of the time. It has a vaguely Latin rhythm with drum breaks and Stu's R&B piano work. It sounds like John is harmonising with Tom here for an Everlys effect, but details are thin, particularly for this final single. The flipside is more of the same, a Tommy Fogerty writing credit. He sings solo on this one.

Tommy Fogerty and The Blue Velvets continued to play shows in the Bay area but did not record again under that name. In 1963, John, Stu, and Doug all graduated from high school with plans to attend college and/or start careers. The band managed to stay together and in 1964, they were signed to a new label and given a new name. Creedence Clearwater Revival was four years away, but the next stage was where the sound, the identity, and, indeed, the power structure would emerge.

The space between 1962 and 1964 was vast. In England, 1963 was Phillip Larkin's 'Annus Mirabilis', bookended by the banning of *Lady Chatterley's Lover* and the release of The Beatles' first album. In America, the assassination of John F Kennedy in November 1963, followed by The Beatles' arrival in New York a couple of months later, had a powerful effect on American life. Decades always take a while to get started. If The Blue Velvets were sonically still in the fifties, their next step would see them responding to the British Invasion.

Before I put too fine a point on the fact that Creedence would never abandon early rock and roll to any great extent, it must be said that The Beatles themselves were hardly iconoclasts. Though they would, of course, go on to push the form into all sorts of new directions, their early records betray the influence of their years playing rockabilly and R&B standards to drunken sailors in Hamburg in the early 1960s. Like the future Creedence, The Beatles' origins were in the late 1950s. Their sound was original and modern in 1963, but it owed a great debt to, among others, Buddy Holly. A similar point could be made about all the early British invasion acts. The American 'garage' bands and pop acts that imitated them were playing an earlier form of American music filtered through British ears. What makes Creedence somewhat exceptional is that far more than most of their contemporaries, they only flirted with The Beatles before settling on the more primal American version of rock and roll that would become their signature.

In the meantime, Tommy Fogerty and the Blue Velvets successfully auditioned for Max Weiss, president of Fantasy Records. Creedence's relationship with the label is a long and complicated story but suffice to say, nobody in 1964 would have imagined that the rock and roll version of Dickens' *Bleak House* was now underway.

Fantasy Records

This label is such an important part of the Creedence story that it is rarely ever mentioned in any other rock and roll context. It began in 1949 and was the first home of Dave Brubeck but not, of course, where he would record his best-known work. In 1955, a young employee called Saul Zaentz married Charles Mingus' ex-wife Celia. As a wedding gift, her first husband handed over Debut Records, a label that he ran with jazz drummer Max Roach, to Fantasy. Among the various recordings on the label was the legendary Jazz At Massey Hall album featuring Mingus, Charlie Parker, Roach, Bud Powell, and Dizzy Gillespie.

Fantasy, from 1958 to 1961, was also the home of the comedian Lenny Bruce whose endless legal troubles foreshadowed those to come for John Fogerty. Fantasy, in the 1950s, also had Cal Tjader and Mongo Santamaria, two extremely influential Latin jazz musicians, on their roster. Tjader would return to the label in the 1970s.

By 1964, record labels the world over – but particularly in the US – were watching the crowds of screaming teenage girls at Beatles concerts and imagining the record sales. The appeal was mysterious to industry veterans. The British music world was an alternative universe with its own stars and trends, none of which had bothered the American charts much until it did. These shaggy kids from England were playing rock and roll, covering musty old songs from the '50s, and generally selling coals to Newcastle. America could surely come up with something better than 'ya ya ya'.

The Blue Velvets would have been an appealing package. They had been playing together for years but were, except for Tom, younger than all The Beatles. They even wrote their own material. They only needed to do something about that name. 'Blue Velvet' was the name of what would have been, in 1964, an extremely unhip hit for Bobby Vinton. The band had probably taken it from The Clovers' 1955 version, but it had to go. They became, at first, The Vision or The Visions, depending on the source.

They were playing the usual gigs at frat parties and military bases in this period, but a residency at a Berkeley dive bar called The Monkey Inn was Creedence's 'Hamburg'. A long residency means that a band has the space and, to avoid boredom, the motivation to change things up, experiment, make a lot of mistakes, and find their sound. It was at The Monkey Inn that John Fogerty began to sing lead. Tom Fogerty recognised that his little brother's voice had a distinctive quality that suited the band. On the singles that followed, Tom slowly gave way to John as lead singer and contented himself with his role as a rhythm guitarist.

The Golliwogs Recordings
'Don't Tell Me No Lies'/'Little Girl (Does Your Mamma Know?)' (Fantasy Records 590)

In the summer of 1964, the band recorded what they thought was a demo at a makeshift studio at the back of the Fantasy office. A few months later, they were invited back to Fantasy and shown a 45 that included 'Don't Tell Me No Lies' as the A-side and 'Little Girl' on the flip. Fantasy was a serious step up from Orchestra and they must have been pleased, at least until they noticed that the songs were credited to The Golliwogs. In what might be the most bizarre of all attempts to cash in on the new appetite for British bands, Max Weiss reached for something he perceived to be terribly English. In fact, the Golliwog character was as American as the four young men scrutinising the record label. It was the creation of Florence Kate Upton, a late 19th-century illustrator and writer from Flushing, New York.

To be fair, her books were extremely well received in England and the character, based on blackface minstrel images, became a popular soft toy there. Enid Blyton used a character called Golliwog in her Noddy books in the 1950s and the toys remained popular well into the 1970s despite the obvious association with racism.

It's difficult to believe that in the middle of the civil rights movement, no one thought it was a dreadful name for a band. There is a notorious group photo with the guys all in white fright wigs that was included in a promo pack for radio stations. Ill-conceived doesn't begin to cover it, but the first single was in the shops.

'Don't Tell Me No Lies' is a convincing attempt to create a Beatles song. The bridge sounds like 1959, but the verses and chorus are pure early Fabs. The song is credited to Rann Wild (Tom) and Toby Green (John), with Tom singing lead. The flipside is closer to the Blue Velvets '50s ballad style, a sound they were quickly leaving behind.

'Where You Been' / 'You Came Walking' (Fantasy 597)
This was the first of two singles to appear in 1965. It is a 1950s-style ballad but with a nod to The Beach Boys. The flipside was another Beatles rewrite, this time in the style of 'Please Please Me'. The guitar work sounds like a distorted version of the Beach Boys' Chuck Berry rip-offs. Listen to John's playing here. Something is stirring and it is only a matter of time!

'You Can't Be True'/'You Got Nothing On Me' (Fantasy 599)
By this point in 1965, The Rolling Stones had arrived. 'Satisfaction' was climbing the charts when this song was recorded, but it sounds more like the Chuck Berry-style twelve-bar blues songs that pepper the Stones' earliest albums. There is adequate harmonica accompaniment and some 'Last Time'-style guitar licks to kick things off. John sings lead here and sounds convincing. For a band that was headed towards a rawer rock and roll style, the Stones were a better model than The Beatles and it is on this single that something of Creedence starts to emerge. The flipside is a 'Roll Over Beethoven' rewrite in a vaguely 'Stones' style. Tom and John both sing on this one.

'Brown-Eyed Girl'/'You Better Be Careful' (Scorpio 404)
A hit! This fourth single, the first of three released in 1966, sold well enough to be released in the UK on Vocalion. It only troubled the local charts in California, but that was enough to reshape the band and set them on their way. John sings lead on the A-side and with Tom on the B-side. The song is not the Van Morrison hit, of course but, ironically, Them's 'Gloria' is the model. This is classic garage and John's familiar rasp is in full flight here. The garage-punk ethic also allows the band to embrace the raw sound more fully, an important step on the road to Creedence. The flipside is akin to The Zombies' 'She's Not There'. It's a great *Nuggets*-style US garage response to the British Invasion.

'Fight Fire'/'Fragile Child' (Scorpio 405)
This single, released in March 1966, is a great favourite of garage music collectors. A step forward for a band developing their sound, it's a three-chord burner with groovy verses. It begins with a distorted guitar lick and chugs along agreeably. It doesn't sound like any particular Creedence song, but the Blue Velvets are a distant memory now and the verses, in particular, make it an obvious precursor to the originals that appear on the first CCR album. Both brothers are credited as writers on the label. 'Fragile Child' is another top garage pop tune. This might be the first single that you could slip onto a CCR compilation without raising too many eyebrows.

'Walking On Water'/'You Better Get It Before It Gets You' (Scorpio 408)
This was their final single of 1966 and the A-side is a great song that was re-recorded for CCR's first album. Though 'Porterville' is officially the first CCR

single, it's difficult not to think of 'Walking On Water' as a real starting point. This version is more beholden to 1966's psychedelic ethos than the better-known 1968 recording, but it is undeniably the sound of the band arriving at something. It has all the swamp menace that will come to define their sound and John Fogerty, all of 21 at this point, sounds like a weathered old bluesman lighting up his first cigarette of the day. The effect for Creedence fans is like Levon and The Hawks' 1965 single 'The Stones That I Throw'. It was all there! The Band only needed to go on tour with Bob Dylan and hang out in a basement with him to get it right. John Fogerty only needs to spend some time marching at Fort Bragg to work out his pathway.

The flipside is worth hearing too. It's a not-so-distant cousin to the Rolling Stones' 'Good Times, Bad Times' but it is an early example of Fogerty using his voice to do something approaching southern soul, albeit via Jagger here.

'Tell Me'/'You Can't Be True' (2nd Version) (Scorpio 410)

This is a phantom single that was only ever a test pressing, released in small numbers. Too bad because it is a righteous slice of garage funk that only saw the light of day when the box set was released in 2001. It's easy to imagine it on the first album. The flipside is an out-take of 'You Can't Be True'.

'Porterville'/'Call It Pretending' (Scorpio 412)

Another phantom release, this is a rare item to the point that there is some argument as to whether it was ever more than a promotional record. Hardcore record collectors debate this point regularly online. In late 1967, Saul Zaentz bought Fantasy Records, the band became Creedence Clearwater Revival and this became their first single. 'Porterville' will be discussed in more detail in the section on the first album, but it fits the bill as both the end of something and the beginning. 'Call It Pretending' is one of the great B-sides. The Four Tops are the source here for this early soul choogle. It deserved a place on the first album but was felt to be too much in their old style to fit into the new vision. It remains the only non-album B-side in the entire Creedence catalogue.

Other assorted songs.

These all appear on the *Fight Fire* compilation

'Try Try Try'

The group in Byrds/Buffalo Springfield mode, this is an interesting song that might have had some success if it had been released.

'Little Tina'

John sings lead on this slightly psychedelic frat rocker. Another cool song that should have been run up the flagpole as a single.

Creedence Clearwater Revival ... *On Track*

'I Only Met You An Hour Ago'

This is a Buddy Holly throwback attempted as an up-tempo Beatles-style song. It's not bad but nothing earth-shattering.

'Gonna Hang Around'

Here's a mode that you don't hear these guys in too often. It's a sort of Smokey and The Miracles groove with a Stax bassline. Worth hearing.

'She Was Mine'

John sings this Animals-style song. I suspect this was recorded in 1965, as you can hear the band trying to fit their early sixties sound into the British Invasion mould here.

The Creedence Sound: Players, Influences, and Precursors

There is no one Creedence sound any more than there is one Rolling Stones sound or a single Beatles style. On every one of their seven albums, CCR experimented with different genres from song to song. Yet there is no mistaking one of their songs when it comes on the radio or a playlist. There is a difference between 'Born on the Bayou', for example, and 'Have You Ever Seen The Rain?' but there is something, a particular quality, that identifies them as CCR songs.

Until their sixth and penultimate release, *Pendulum*, few other instruments are heard on Creedence albums. The 'Buddy Holly' formula – two guitars, bass, drums – is all that you are hearing on the majority of their 60 or so songs. By late 1960s standards, that qualified as minimalist in rock and roll and it set them apart. John Fogerty was a versatile and inventive guitar player, but he couldn't have created the range of Creedence sounds alone.

The Players
Doug Clifford, drums
He is an underrated drummer and a key part of the Creedence sound. In 2013, John Fogerty recorded several Creedence songs with other acts for an album called *Wrote A Song For Everyone*. It has some charming moments, but I defy you to listen to any of the songs without feeling an immediate need to hear the original. There is something about Clifford and Fogerty's chemistry that is missing in the updated versions. Clifford was never only a timekeeper. He's following Fogerty's vocal and lead guitar work at every step. There are great drummers and there are drummers who listen. Clifford is the latter. His timing, his ability to play rockabilly rhythms, and his poignant rolls are all integral.

Stu Cook, bass
His bass work is also underrated. Cook grew into the job. He was always a rock-solid part of the rhythm section, but by the *Willie and the Poor Boys* LP, a much more melodic side begins to emerge. Stu never overplays. He is part of that elite group in rock and roll of 'smart' bass players. Like Clifford, he is a listener who locates his place in the arrangement. He can fill it up or he can step back. The rockabilly style comes naturally, but he also shines on the R&B material and the more acoustic songs. Listen to the *Pendulum* album on headphones with the bass turned up slightly. There is a lot going on.

Tom Fogerty, rhythm guitar
What was wonderful about Tom Fogerty's guitar work was that he took his title seriously, meaning he wasn't the frustrated second guitarist, riffing and slyly slipping in bits of lead work. He was part of the rhythm section. His style is a key element in their sound. Sometimes he is playing in tandem with

John, sometimes, he's quietly providing gentle up strokes way down in the mix. Creedence's arrangements never sound busy or crowded. If he had been a different kind of player, they might have sounded, guitar-wise, more like Buffalo Springfield or even the Stones. There is no gladiatorial axe battle here. Like the others in the rhythm section, Tom used space rather than simply filling it.

John Fogerty, guitar, voice, harmonica, keys, saxophone

John Fogerty's voice should be in the Smithsonian. It's powerful, evocative, and utterly American. Part Howlin' Wolf, Wilson Pickett, Rick Nelson, Hank Williams and part gospel preacher, it's not a 'beautiful' voice or one that would get all three judges on their feet on one of those singing shows. He's a storyteller, a campfire orator. It's a weary, weathered instrument that developed in the mid-sixties while the band chased success. Night after night in California dive bars, his original voice broke down and gave way to something new. No one sounds like John Fogerty.

His guitar playing is striking too. While many of his contemporaries were based in the various Chicago blues styles, he was, at heart, a rockabilly player in the tradition of Scotty Moore. Blues is certainly in there – Albert King, in particular – but so is Steve Cropper's work at Stax, Pop Staples' reverb gospel lines, Duane Eddy's hillbilly surf, and James Burton's classy work with Rick Nelson.

Influences and Precursors
Rockabilly

Two words: Scotty Moore. He was Elvis' original guitar player and one of the architects of rockabilly and rock and roll guitar. He picked up where early figures like Charlie Christian, Merle Travis and Sister Rosetta Tharpe left off, and created a template for lead playing that remains in use. John Fogerty has never made any secret of his admiration for the man. In countless guitar magazine interviews, he has raved about the older guitarist's work on Elvis's early recordings. The cover of 'My Baby Left Me' on *Cosmo's Factory* is almost a note-for-note re-creation of the King's 1956 version. Presley's recordings at Sun Records left their mark on Fogerty, but if you are searching for one of the main ingredients in the Creedence sound, it is closer to those early RCA sessions with drummer DJ Fontana joining Scotty, Bill Black, and Elvis. 'My Baby Left Me' was one of the first recordings Elvis made after leaving Sun.

Rockabilly is one of the great postmodern forms. It has fragments of blues, boogie woogie piano, bluegrass, hillbilly bop, western swing, rhythm and blues, and even bebop jazz. Sometimes, it is mistakenly called 'an early form of rock and roll'. This suggests that it went out with pedal pushers and hula hoops. A cursory listen to popular rock and roll in the following decades suggests that it is never far below the surface. When The Stray Cats had hit singles in the early 1980s, there was talk of a 'revival'. I'm not sure that it needed reviving. That would be ignoring the rockabilly songs recorded by The Beatles and other British Invasion bands in the 1960s, along with obvious nods to the form in so much garage punk. CCR bridged the late 1960s and early 1970s, in time for the obvious rockabilly elements in glam. Consider David Essex's 'Rock On' or Mud's 'The Cat Crept In'. Punk always seemed to have rockabilly somewhere in the mix and American bands like X, The Gun Club, and, of course, The Cramps just made it obvious. Among the early English punk bands, The Sex Pistols, The Clash and The Jam all recorded rockabilly standards. At about the same time, Bruce Springsteen was doing things like 'Open All Night' in his basement in New Jersey. These are a few random examples, but my point is that it was a form distinct from early rock and roll and remains so.

It's been noted that Creedence was out of step with their exact contemporaries in the San Francisco music scene of the 1960s. The fact that rockabilly rather than blues underpinned their sound is significant. Most of the other San Francisco bands associated with that period were staffed with either blues players or ex-folkies. Geography comes into play here as Creedence's early days as The Blue Velvets were spent playing scout halls and Junior High dances in the suburbs like the one they had grown up in. Country Joe MacDonald, after a spell in the army, ended up in Berkeley. It was a short bus ride from El Cerrito where the Creedence guys grew up but, culturally, was another universe. The university and a long bohemian tradition meant that Berkeley would be one staging ground for the West Coast folk revival. Jerry Garcia moved around the city as a child but spent his formative years as a musician in Menlo Park, which, like Berkeley, had a nearby university – Stanford – and a bohemian element where folk music was the soundtrack. Joan Baez finished high school and began her music career in the area. Country Joe and Jerry were early rock and roll fans too, but while they were learning Leadbelly songs to play at the local coffee house in 1960, John Fogerty was polishing up the latest Duane Eddy instrumental for a prom in El Cerrito.

Fogerty provides a comprehensive list of influences in his memoir, *Fortunate Son* (2015). Rockabilly favourites include Rick Nelson's early work with the legendary James Burton on guitar and Carl Perkins, who was also an influence on George Harrison. His preference seemed to be for the more countrified version of rockabilly. Fellow Californian Eddie Cochran is not mentioned, nor is Gene Vincent. Fogerty lists some lesser-known names, too. Jimmy Dee and the Offbeats' 'Henrietta' is a gutbucket Texas rockabilly workout that he has covered in his solo career. If you listen past the hiccupping vocals, there is something of the Creedence choogle here. Fogerty wasn't the only one who loved this record. There is some evidence that it was the first single a certain teenager in Hibbing, Minnesota, bought and learned to play before going acoustic in 1960.

'Endless Sleep' by Jody Reynolds is another song that Fogerty returns to several times in his memoir. Reynolds grew up in Oklahoma and had a brief period in the spotlight when this song climbed the national charts in 1958. The reverb-laden guitar in the first few bars turns up in more than a few Creedence songs and it isn't difficult to imagine them covering it. Intriguingly, The Gun Club, who ably tackled Creedence's 'Run Through The Jungle' in the 1980s, recorded Reynolds' 'Fire Of Love' for their second album and named their first after it.

There was a craze for guitar instrumentals in the late fifties that left its mark on Fogerty. Duane Eddy, whose 'Rebel Rouser' was a smash hit, is one example, but the titan of guitar instrumentals, Link Wray, must have also played some part. Fogerty mentions Chuck Berry's 1957 instrumental, 'Deep Feeling', in his memoir, too.

Rhythm and Blues

Rockabilly is an obvious influence, but Creedence also recorded songs by Wilson Pickett, Ray Charles, Marvin Gaye, and Screamin' Jay Hawkins. John Fogerty's admiration for Booker T and the MGs is well documented and I will cover this in more detail later. In his memoir, he mentions Bobby Blue Bland's Little Boy Blue and Jerry Butler and The Impressions' 'For Your Precious Love'. Both reveal their own gospel influences suggesting that Fogerty leaned in that direction in his R&B tastes. Bland's growling delivery is an influence too. He also mentions 'I Confess' by The Four Rivers, another gospel-tinged rhythm and blues song. In terms of actual gospel, anyone who has heard 'Uncloudy Day' by The Staples Singers knows that Pop Staples' guitar playing is in the Fogerty mix too.

Folk

One of the factors that contributed to the flowering of so much great rock and roll in the mid to late '60s was the folk revival that took place in the late 1950s. Bluegrass, jug bands, pre-war blues, ragtime, Appalachian music, protest songs, music from around the world, and whatever could be played on acoustic instruments and signified authenticity came under the banner of 'folk' for a few years in between the decline of the first wave of rockers and the appearance of The Beatles. In political terms, it was linked with a rising wave of activism around civil rights and the opposition to the proliferation of nuclear weapons.

Woody Guthrie, a figure of the 1930s who wrote 'This Land Is Your Land' as a not-so-subtle left-wing response to 'God Bless America' was, by the late '50s, ill with Huntington's disease but existed as a sort of focal point for the revival of American 'roots' music. Bob Dylan, a young rock and roller who was converted to folk by Guthrie's memoir, famously hitchhiked to New York to meet the man himself and sing his songs in dingy cafes in Greenwich Village. To some extent, Bob caught the tail end of something that had begun in the '50s with singers like Odetta, Harry Belafonte, and the Kingston Trio. Greenwich Village was filled with earnest young Guthrie clones singing ballads and sea shanties. Woody's old friend Pete Seeger presided over the folk revival as an elder while continuing to stage entertaining shows and put out interesting records.

Many of the American acts that appeared in the mid-1960s had their roots in the folk revival. The Grateful Dead began as a jug band, The Byrds' Gene Clark spent time in the New Christy Minstrels, John Sebastian had been in the Even Dozen Jug Band. Janis Joplin had a coffee house past. Creedence did not, as it happened, but John Fogerty acknowledges the impact that the folk revival had on his musical imagination in his memoir. He attended festivals in California and declares Pete Seeger the greatest entertainer he's ever seen.

Creedence is rarely mentioned when the subject of 'folk rock' comes up and, indeed, their first album appeared after the original boom had faded. It might have been more obvious if they had recorded an entire LP in the mid-1960s, but the folk influence remains on their cover of Leadbelly's 'Midnight Special' and the concept behind *Willie and The Poor Boys*. Similarly, the protest element in songs like 'Bad Moon Rising', 'Have You Ever Seen The Rain?', 'Fortunate Son' and others is a result of a turn towards the topical in folk songwriting. The fact that Fogerty avoided love songs in the Creedence days suggests the influence of folk. Rockabilly, as a form, is almost exclusively concerned with romantic topics. If Creedence was indeed a neo-rockabilly band, they were so in sound only.

Country

In 1981, Fantasy brought out a compilation called *Creedence Country* with some idea of either interesting country artists in the songs or somehow getting on country radio. Little of the material is 'country' as such, but country music does indeed inform Creedence's sound. John Fogerty's first post-CCR release was an album called *Blue Ridge Rangers* that included covers of songs made famous by Hank Williams, George Jones, Webb Pierce, Hank Locklin, and Merle Haggard. He did not stumble onto this music in 1973.

Country music had a significant impact on rock and roll in the late 1960s. The Byrds' *Sweetheart of the Rodeo*, Dylan's *Nashville Skyline*, and the Beau Brummels' *Bradley's Barn* cleared the way for the country rock phenomenon. An obvious source of this movement was not the 'Nashville sound' of the early sixties, but the much harder-edged California-based Bakersfield twang of groups like The Maddox Brothers and Rose and, famously, Buck Owens and His Buckaroos. These bands drew on the Hillbilly Bop of the late '40s, rockabilly, Western swing and rock and roll for a sound that had great appeal to fans who found the lush Nashville productions of Owen Bradley and Chet Atkins too mannered. John Fogerty has regularly mentioned Don Rich, the Buckaroos guitarist, as an influence. Rich usually played a Telecaster through a Fender Bassman amplifier for a distinctively clean sound that Fogerty imitated regularly in CCR. For a quick reference point, The Buckaroos instrumental 'Buckaroo' is a good place to see how important Rich was to Fogerty.

Blues

While there is no Creedence blues compilation to go with the country one, there is an album of covers called 'A Blues Tribute to Creedence Clearwater Revival' from 2001 that does reveal the degree to which blues figure in the band's sound. They were never an obvious contender for the 'blues rock' label, but like the guitarists in those bands, John Fogerty's playing and approach to soloing was informed by players like Howlin Wolf's guitarist Hubert Sumlin, Buddy Guy, in his earliest work with Muddy Waters, Freddie King, along with minimalists like Jimmy Reed and Slim Harpo. In his memoir, Fogerty mentions Lightning Hopkins too. As with country, Fogerty was drawn to the rawer, more elemental sounds of this genre.

Creedence Clearwater Revival (1968)

Personnel:
Doug Clifford: drums
Stu Cook: bass
Tom Fogerty: rhythm guitar
John Fogerty: guitar, voice, harmonica
Recorded: October 1967 & February 1968, Coast Recorders, Hollywood
Released: May 1968
Label: Fantasy
Producer: John Fogerty, Saul Zaentz
Running Time: 33:17
Highest Chart Position: US 52, UK did not chart

The first Creedence single was 'Porterville' backed with 'Call It Pretending'. Saul Zaentz's disagreements with John Fogerty are now part of rock and roll mythology but in late 1967, they were of one mind about one thing: The Golliwogs was a terrible name for a band. John had returned from a stint in the military with a new approach to songwriting – more about this soon – and a record company now owned by someone he considered a friend, Saul Zaentz. It was time for a new name and an LP.

The name, which sounds like it means a lot more than it does came from three sources. Credence (they added an extra e) was the name of someone's friend. Clearwater was inspired by an advertisement for Olympia Beer who were making a big deal about the water they employed for brewing in their marketing at the time. Revival came from a sense that the band, now nearly ten years old was going to be reborn with a new name and a new direction. The time for 'The Something Plurals' was over and Jefferson Airplane were the most successful band in San Francisco at the time. Creedence Clearwater Revival was a name for 1968.

And 1968 was, even by sixties standards, an explosive twelve months of music. I don't want to overstate this point because I suspect a similar case could be made for any year in music from 1965 to 1973, but the acts that released their debut albums in this year do seem to suggest the beginning of something. In addition to CCR, The Band released *Music From Big Pink*. Both acts signalled a move away from psychedelia and a return to American forms – country, r&b, blues. Neither act is overly indebted to The Beatles or The Rolling Stones and this is significant. In The Band's case, they would soon be the main influence on a whole group of British musicians, including Fairport Convention, Eric Clapton, and, yes, The Beatles.

Another debut in 1968 was Dr John's *Gris Gris*, a creation of studio player Mac Rebenack. If it was psychedelic, it was an American version. The landscape was more Bayou Teche than Wild Wood and the magic was more Marie Laveau than Madame Blavatsky. Rebenack, unlike John Fogerty, was actually from Louisiana, but they both seemed to arrive at some sort of swamp rock epiphany in the same year. It should be noted that 'Polk Salad Annie' by Tony Joe White was released in 1969 but recorded in May of the previous year. Trying to establish a starting point for any music genre is a fool's game, but I will propose 1968 as year zero for Swampedelia.

Their first album is sometimes seen as the product of a band discovering its sound with all the attendant pitfalls associated with experimentation. It's true to some extent and I will discuss Fogerty's deliberate shot at airplay with 'Suzie Q'. But it is also sometimes seen as a weak first attempt and when CCR records are ranked, it is always at the number six spot, above the seriously flawed final effort *Mardi Gras*. Trying to rank this band's excellent catalogue is difficult, but the automatic consignment of their first album to second worst is misguided. Yes, it is raw and yes, it stumbles at points, but it is also an exhilarating snapshot of a great band taking flight. With nearly a decade of flop singles and sticky carpet gigs behind them, they have nothing to live up to and everything to prove. So I will say that this is a seriously underrated album.

It was certainly underrated by Barry Gifford in Rolling Stone. The novelist and all-around man of letters is impressed by John Fogerty but not the rest of the band. He declared them better live but concluded by saying he wasn't sure the revival was worth it – ha ha. A local jazz player is quoted as saying that he'd rather listen to an old man cough than CCR's rhythm section. Really? In hindsight, it reads like a premature dismissal of a band that would soon be selling a lot more records than any other San Francisco act but, seeing as he only had the first album at hand, the recognition that John Fogerty had something special is worth noting. It's one of those negative reviews where one can see a sliver of doubt in the writer about his poor opinion of the album.

The album was recorded quickly and astonishingly cheaply at Coast Recorders in San Francisco. Saul Zaentz is listed as the producer, but, as John Fogerty always quickly points out, he had nothing to do with the production. The first album is a collaboration between a confident 22-year-old with a string of largely unsuccessful singles behind him and Walt Payne, the engineer they had met years earlier as James Powell's backing band. John Fogerty seemed to know exactly what sound he wanted. Payne, who had engineered albums by The Smothers Brothers and Liberace, showed him a few tricks to get it.

On this first album, Creedence developed an approach to recording that they maintained until *Pendulum* in 1970. The key was preparation. The songs were arranged and rehearsed so that they could get a good take in three to five run-throughs. This, as any student of late '60s rock and roll knows, was not what bands were doing by this point. This old-school approach guaranteed a degree of freshness on the tracks. The first album was recorded on a four-track live but with the vocals added later. For Fogerty, who mixed the album, it was all about the live sound. He was not interested in smoothing any rough edges or applying a clear finish. The ideal was Chess Records' early Howlin Wolf sides or Otis Redding's recordings on Stax. The band needed to sound powerful, not slick.

Aside from a deliberate capitulation on 'Suzie Q', that I will come to, Creedence's first album doesn't suggests any affinity with The Grateful Dead, Jefferson Airplane, Quicksilver Messenger Service, Moby Grape, or indeed any other San Francisco band at the time. So why was CCR so different?

There are plenty of theories, but John Fogerty's personality comes into play. In a period where there was an emphasis on individual expression and 'doing one's own thing', this young man never showed the least interest in following the example of his contemporaries in San Francisco. His models were rockabilly artists from the previous decade along with Southern acts like Booker T and the MGs. His stint in the military meant that he spent the summer of love marching instead of hanging around Haight Ashbury. He was not interested in psychedelics and had no patience with the philosophy of 'tune in, turn on, and drop out.' In his memoir, he calls Timothy Leary a 'buffoon'. CCR were not unaware of their fellow San Francisco bands. In 1968, they were playing at venues in the city like the Carousel, the Avalon Ballroom, and the Fillmore. They shared bills with It's a Beautiful Day, Steppenwolf and the Dead. It seemed to have no effect on them. This is not to say that all the San Francisco bands sounded the same except for CCR. It's more like an aesthetic or approach that ties bands like Country Joe and the Fish together with Big Brother and the Holding Company. They were innovating, testing the limits, and applying the improvisatory ideas of free jazz to blues-based rock and roll. This was not what Creedence was doing. On this first album, at least, Creedence was establishing something that was by no means anachronistic but was firmly based in a pre-Pepper world.

Ted Hughes wrote that literature is 'to some extent the voice of what is neglected or forbidden, hence its connection to the past in the nostalgic vein, and the future in the revolutionary vein'. On their first album, this could function as something of a mission statement. The biggest hit on the album was a ten-year-old rockabilly song, but the album as a whole formed the basis of a radical and soon-to-be popular approach to the rock and roll form.

'I Put A Spell On You' (Jalacy Hawkins)

Leaving aside 'Porterville', their first single as Creedence, for the moment, this is how they introduced themselves to the world in May of 1968. John Fogerty has said that he regarded the cover versions on the early Stones and Beatles records as statements about their commitment to rock and roll and as resume items. 'See what we can do with Chuck Berry? Wait until you hear our songs'. One has the impression that on this first CCR album, they were making a similar statement.

The various covers are not from the standard 1960s repertoire. No Chuck Berry, no Sonny Boy Williamson, no Carl Perkins, and no Buddy Holly songs appeared on this or any other CCR album. Instead, we get Dale Hawkins, Wilson Pickett, and Screamin' Jay Hawkins. A more obvious take on a Bo Diddley song was left off for reasons I will come to at the end of this section.

Screamin' Jay's original of 'I Put A Spell On You' was the result of a drunken recording session that included, in addition to Hawkins, guitarist Mickey Baker and tenor saxophonist, Sam 'The Man' Taylor. The result was something between spooky and comic. Jalacy 'Jay' Hawkins bellows and grunts over top of a triplet-based arrangement that is spare but effective. Hawkins sounds desperate but also a bit nuts. Alan Freed, the legendary New York DJ, saw the potential immediately and put Hawkins on the stage in a coffin surrounded by dubious shrunken voodoo heads. Arguably, it was the first in a long series of horror-themed rock and roll novelty songs and it remains a much-loved classic from the early days of the form.

It was hardly a lost gem by the time CCR recorded it 12 years later. By that point, there had been numerous covers, including well-known takes by Nina Simone and Alan Price of The Animals. About a month after CCR released their first album, The Crazy World of Arthur Brown's debut included an organ-drenched version.

Nina Simone's 1965 version extracted the pathos of the original without the theatrics. Alan Price followed suit but gave it a faster, more rhythmic groove with a full horn section. Creedence focussed on atmosphere. The opening few seconds sound like eerie church bells before Doug Clifford's parade ground roll opens the song for real. Tom Fogerty's rhythm guitar sets up the groove as John strums open chords and begins to sing.

The song was a recent addition to the band's setlist though they must have all known it well. It's a great showcase for growling wolf vocals and the band's low-end choogle style. The obvious choice here was something like 'Smokestack Lightning' for a minor blues workout, but the fact that 'I Put A Spell On You' is more associated with rock and roll is significant. Blues is a factor on this record, as we will see, but Fogerty's vision for Creedence was based in early rock and roll.

Considering that they were just getting started, Creedence's version of 'I Put A Spell On You' is a powerful and ominous track. John's swirling lead guitar, Stu's solid bass work and Doug's melodic drumming, along with Tom's steady rhythm guitar work, all knit together seamlessly. These guys had been playing together for a long time. A lot of these songs were done in a take or two. The chemistry is obvious and this is a great start to the album. They must have liked it, too, as it remained in their live shows for the next couple of years, notably the one at Yasgur's farm in 1969.

'The Working Man' (John Fogerty)

John Fogerty continued to broaden his topical range as a songwriter as the band prepared to record their first album. In this blues-based track, he takes the voice of the eponymous character for a deceptively simple set of lyrics. The line – 'born on a Sunday, on Thursday I had me a job' was, roughly speaking, part of a long 'work song' tradition going back hundreds of years. That somewhat vague label covers everything from sea shanties and slavery era songs to industrial folk songs but all deal with the topic of work. Some of the songs grew out of a need to pass the time doing dull tasks and others were a way to blow off steam with a litany of complaints about the pay, the boss, the conditions, etc. John Fogerty's working man has been so busy that he hasn't had time to get into trouble. He also asks that he not die on Friday because that's payday. He'd rather go on a Saturday, so he doesn't have to face his hangover on Sunday. This slightly wry commentary is in keeping with the tradition but it's significant that his first original album track is concerned with working-class life.

Much has been made of the band's affinity with working-class fans and I will certainly pick this point up again. But this song is important because it was written as Fogerty was formulating a new approach to songwriting. 'Porterville', as we will see, had convinced him that he should tell stories that weren't about falling in or out of love. It is thus notable that one of his early efforts was something of a tribute to the 'worker'.

Some reviews suggest that, musically, 'The Working Man' is indebted to Howlin Wolf. The main riff, a nifty minor run, and the blues guitar colour added by John throughout the song, gives it a Chicago blues feel, but there is something of Albert King and the more funky Texas blues tradition here too. It isn't a straight blues but more the sort of 'chooglin'' tune that would come to define a component of their sound.

'Suzie Q' (Dale Hawkins, Eleanor Broadwater, Stanley Lewis)

The original version of this song was recorded at a radio station in Shreveport, Louisiana in 1957. The singer and principal author of the song was a young rockabilly singer called Dale Hawkins. The guitar player and riff auteur on the song was seventeen-year-old James Burton, who would go on to play with Ricky Nelson and later Elvis Presley. His early work with Nelson represents the cream of rockabilly guitar work but this early effort might be his masterpiece. There is, to my ears, no discernible bass player on this track, so Burton builds a bassline into the riff, a variation on the standard open position run in E that can be heard on so many blues records. The drummer bashes away and Hawkins sings the lyrics. The lack of a bass and the defining blues riff mean that it is only a rockabilly song by the widest definition. Hawkins envisioned something that sounded like Elvis, but Burton turns it into something new, a Louisiana blues style of rockabilly that would come to be known as swamp rock. There is nothing particularly surprising about CCR covering Dale Hawkins' song. Everything about the original, the raw recording, the killer country blues riff, and the attack of Hawkins' vocals would have appealed to them. In the context of this album and the band's sound in general, one has the sense that if this song hadn't existed, they would have had to invent it.

Creedence was not, of course, the first group to cover it. The Rolling Stones featured a frantic version on their first album. The Trashmen found the creepy aspect in their singular 1965 take on the song. In 1964, Ronnie Hawkins

(Dale's cousin) released an album called *Mojo Men* that contained a version of the song. I have no idea if John Fogerty was aware of Ronnie's cover, but he also slowed it down and swung it slightly. If you are interested in what it sounds like without the riff and little smell of swamp, Bobby Vee recorded a pop version in 1961. Johnny Rivers folded it into his somewhat generic sound too at some point in the mid-sixties.

In his memoir, *Fortunate Son*, John Fogerty gives considerable space to 'Suzie Q' (CCR changed the spelling of the song slightly) and provides some insights into its creation. He mentions that he imagined something closer to a gospel-style shuffle rhythm than the staccato rockabilly beat of the original. They had been playing the song for as long as it had been around, but his memoir suggests that the recording, which would be the first single released after the album appeared in May 1968, was built from the ground up. It was part of the 'revival' that John Fogerty imagined when he came out of the military and the band changed its name. He has said that this song helped to define Creedence.

It's difficult to know how much of this is retrospective but Fogerty says that he was trying to make a statement with something he considered a simple song. The Beatles had created something of a monster with *Sgt Pepper's Lonely Hearts Club Band*, in his view, and now rock and roll had become far too cerebral. 'Suzie Q' was his response. He says that it was a 'gutbucket, country blues thing. And people liked it.' As I have noted, 1968 saw a few acts reaching back for something less adorned, The Beatles included.

That said, there was nothing retro about an eight-and-a-half-minute song featuring a long guitar workout, a chorus section with freaky compressed 'telephone' vocals, odd background chanting, a swinging '60s bass line, and a sort of 'Day In The Life' crescendo starting just before the eight-minute mark. This ain't rockabilly! But John Fogerty didn't imagine it was. He had one ambition for this song and that was to get it played on KSAN, the legendary San Francisco station that would later broadcast a four-hour symposium on the Altamont Festival disaster. KSAN was part of the new 'free form' FM format that was moving away from the Top 40 format by playing 'deep cuts' and long-form live jams. Fogerty mentions Paul Butterfield's 'East/West', a blues raga and title song from their second album, as the sort of thing he had in mind.

'Suzie Q' is one of Creedence's great moments, but more than that, it is a masterclass in covering a song properly. Unless you are actively deconstructing the original – Nick Cave's version of Leonard Cohen's 'Tower of Song' comes to mind – there is a balance to be struck between holding onto whatever it was that made the song worth covering in the first place while at the same time making something new out of it. Leaving aside the 'psychedelic' aspects of it, the use of a shuffle beat along with a funky bassline while retaining the swamp blues elements is nothing short of electrifying.

After nearly ten years together, they came within a hair of the national top ten with the single, which cleverly featured the more AM radio-friendly half of the song on one side. At four-plus minutes, it was long but could be faded at several points. Part Two was the trippier part of the song for the more adventurous listeners and programmers. It remains one of their most loved songs.

'Ninety Nine and a Half Won't Do' (Eddie Floyd, Wilson Pickett, Steve Cropper)

This is another cover, of course, but one from a much better-known artist at the time, Wilson Pickett. His original was released as a single (b/w 'Danger Zone') in 1966 and peaked at 53 on the Billboard charts, his least successful 45 in a stellar year of 'Mustang Sally', 'Land of 1000 Dances', and '634-5789'. It also appeared that year on one of the great soul LPs, *The Exciting Wilson Pickett*. The tracks that make up the Pickett album are divided between those recorded with the Swampers at Muscle Shoals and those done at Stax with Booker T and the MGs. So, yes, it's a pretty good album.

'Ninety Nine and a Half Won't Do' was one of the Stax recordings. John Fogerty has never made any secret of his admiration for Booker T and the MGs. In his memoir, he calls them the 'greatest rock and roll band' noting that they 'say a lot with a little'. He says that they were Creedence's idols and that he was consciously imitating MGs' guitarist Steve Cropper regularly in those days. Earlier in the memoir, he mentions the 1967 Stax album that Albert King recorded with the MGs, *Born Under A Bad Sign*, as an influence on CCR's sound.

They weren't the first to cover it. Wilson Pickett's raw recordings were appealing to garage bands throughout the US and covering one of his songs became obligatory. The Doors can be heard ploughing through his 'Don't Fight It' on the *London Fog 1966* live recording and their LA contemporaries, The Standells – best known for the song, 'Dirty Water' – released a cover of 'Ninety Nine and Half Won't Do' on the B-side of their 1967 single, 'Can't Help But Love You'. Their cover is looser than CCR's.

For John Fogerty, one has the impression that he was reaching for something in his vocals and this song provided an opportunity to stretch out. He is imitating Pickett to some extent but, as is the case when one seeks to imitate, something new is created. In this case, it is the raspy weapon he will employ on the title track of the next album to great effect.

This song wasn't released as a single but remained a presence in their setlists for the next couple of years. A live version can be heard on the *Live At Woodstock* album.

'Get Down Woman' (John Fogerty)

This is the least inspired track on an otherwise solid record. Hank Bordowitz, in his band biography, *Bad Moon Rising*, suggests that it is an attempt at a BB King-style blues song. To me, it sounds like a twelve-bar jam with more or less improvised lyrics. It isn't terrible, just not terribly interesting. John

Fogerty's increasingly confident lead playing is on display here and the band is solid behind him. It was early days, but the band had discovered how to record John's vocals. The album was recorded at Coast Recorders and Fogerty mentions working with Ward Payne, the same engineer they had met as James Powell's backing band years earlier. Fogerty's voice is distinctive and needs space. Somehow, he learned early how to get his voice right on record. If there is one thing that characterises a lot of first albums in some uncertainty about where to put the singer in the mix. 'Get Down Woman' is a tad predictable, but the vocals are exactly where they should be – no minor accomplishment on a first album!

'Porterville' (John Fogerty)

This is a significant song in the Creedence story for several reasons. The first is that it began as the final Golliwogs 45 before it was issued as the first Creedence Clearwater Revival single. The second is that, for John Fogerty, it represented a shift in his writing away from romantic musings toward narrative songs. Topical songs had been part of the folk revival and often involved stories or parables. Bob Dylan, in his early years as a folk singer, wrote songs like 'The Ballad of Hollis Brown' where he related the sad tale of a North Dakota farmer driven to a desperate act. The Beatles, as they shifted from hand-holding and eight-day weeks, created characters like 'Eleanor Rigby' and the 'Nowhere Man'. The Rolling Stones, The Who, and The Kinks had all left 'Moons' and 'Junes' behind too by this point.

John Fogerty's damascene moment came while he was on active duty in the military reserves in 1967. To avoid the draft, he enlisted in the army. This sounds counterintuitive but it wasn't an uncommon move in the US in the mid-sixties. By enlisting, he was able to maintain some control over his military career. It was risky, but it meant that he wasn't automatically in line for active duty like those who were drafted. He was in the reserves for almost two years, which meant regular training periods at bases all over the US. At one of these, while marching around the same parade ground in the heat for several hours, he started to think of a story. It was about an outsider, a man suffering because of his father's reputation who is forced to run from the town where he grew up. The marching then became a rock-solid 4/4 beat to which he began, in his head presumably, to write lyrics that told the story. 'Porterville' is a small town in the San Joaquin Valley in California, but it could have been any small town. He never mentions the name in the song, but it works better than calling it 'Small Town'.

The narrator in the song begins by stating he hasn't been back to his hometown for a long time and that he wouldn't risk it because 'the things they said when I was young / are quite enough to get me hung.' It's not 'Folsom Prison Blues' or 'Friend of the Devil'. We don't know if any of the things are true, only that they are believed by the townspeople. In the second verse, it turns out that he hasn't done anything, but his father has, and it is thought that he is cut of the same cloth. Theodore Louis Trost, in his essay, 'Devil's on the Loose: Creedence Clearwater Revival and the Religious Imagination' groups together a number of songs which he terms origin stories – i.e. songs about where the character came from. 'Green River' is the best known but 'Porterville' is an early example. The town he describes could be Porterville, California in the mid-century or it could be an Old Testament-era village in the Negev where the sins of the father are visited on the sons. Or, according to John Fogerty, it could have been the landscape of one of Tennessee Williams' plays. It's not clear which one, but it could be *Orpheus Descending* which was made into a film starring Marlon Brando called *The Fugitive Kind* in 1960.

John Fogerty says, intriguingly, that 'Porterville' is about how he regards the world and where he is 'coming from', presumably meaning that in a figurative way. Leaving his autobiography aside, this story of the outsider or exile is worth considering. In America in 1968, a lot of people were asking themselves where 'home,' or the America that they knew, had gone. The Vietnam War was divisive enough to undermine ideas of right and wrong and this was reflected in films like *The Graduate* and books like Truman Capote's *In Cold Blood*. It also, as we will see, became a prominent theme in Fogerty's stories.

With some imagination, it's easy to hear something of the parade ground in the sound of 'Porterville'. The medium-tempo rhythm is something one can march to and the stinging guitar riff that opens the song sounds like a bugle. It's a simple but inventively arranged chord progression that sees Stu and Doug continuing to develop the rumbling bottom-end bass drum combination that is such an important part of the CCR sound.

'Porterville' was not, after the success of 'Suzie Q', a feature of their live shows and it remains relatively unknown among their songs. It does, however, represent a watershed moment for John Fogerty as a songwriter. It appears in Sean Penn's 2007 film, *Into The Wild*, a film about outsiders, if there ever was one.

'Gloomy' (John Fogerty)

Again, one of the most compelling aspects of this album is the 'work in progress' status of John Fogerty's musical imagination and the band's sound. The lyrics to 'Gloomy' are not particularly profound, a series of standard observations about life concluding that everything is, well, gloomy. The more compelling part of the song are the obvious influences and the production.

Unlike The Stones, The Yardbirds, The Doors, and countless other rock and roll bands of the 1960s, Creedence did not cover a Howlin' Wolf song. However, their sound is as permeated by Wolf's music as those that did. Fogerty mentions his admiration for the older bluesman several times in his memoir, noting that he had trouble processing the fact that Wolf was supporting CCR at a show. 'He looked at me as though he was going to reach down and pat me on the head'.

Chester 'Howlin' Wolf' Burnett, like his rival and contemporary Muddy Waters, began his career in the south before moving to Chicago during the 'great migration' of African Americans to the more industrialised northern US. In the '30s, he knew and had played with legendary figures like Charley Patton, Son House, and even Robert Johnson. He brought the Delta sound with him. His Chess Records recordings, like those of Muddy Waters, evoke the mythical elements of the south. Hints of voodoo and the supernatural appear in his lyrics. Wolf's songs had a profound influence on John Fogerty.

But the sound is important too. The electrified Delta blues guitar style of Wolf's long-time sideman, Hubert Sumlin, repeatedly appears on Creedence albums. It is also obvious that along with Wilson Pickett, Howlin' Wolf is one of the singers that Fogerty drew on for his own growling vocals.

But Gloomy also features backwards guitar sounds and other assorted noises courtesy of John Fogerty's young son's wind-up toys. Somewhere, right before the two-minute mark, the tempo changes and the song kicks into something that sounds much more like the 'San Francisco sound'. Fogerty plays an extended and slightly psychedelic solo to finish things up about 90 seconds later. It may have been another tilt at KSAN's playlists. One of John Fogerty's guiding principles was that whatever was done in the studio needed to be able to be performed on stage. The use of studio tricks here suggests that he had something in mind for this one.

Indeed, it did not appear in the band's live sets after their stint at Dino and Carlo's. A cover by a Finnish band, The Barefoot Brothers, is worth tracking down.

'Walk on the Water' (John Fogerty, Tom Fogerty)

Hands up if you bought Richard Hell and the Voidoids' album *Blank Generation* as a teenager and did a double-take when you noticed the writing credit on this song. Richard Hell successfully makes it sound like a late-night in Alphabet City. In a Finnish language version Kari Peitsamo turns it into an earnest folk song. The Wave Pictures featuring Billy Childish reach back to the original for a punk/psych take with harmonica. The Brandos' proto-grunge workout from 1987 completes the set.

Of course, Creedence were covering themselves when they recorded this one for their first album. The Golliwogs were never better than on this 1966 single and if CCR had never existed, you'd be crawling across glass for more music by these guys. As I noted in that section, it is the first single that points to the future for them.

The 1968 Creedence version loses the 1966 jingle jangle and the Buffalo Springfield-style guitar solo. The drums are heavier here and the sound is generally tougher. The guitar solo is more in the 'Suzie Q' line and Stu is opening up more on bass. In terms of genre, the version on this album is far closer to the blues psych of 1968 than the psych folk of the original, more *Vincebus Eruptus* than *Da Capo*.

The lyrics are brief but intriguing. John Fogerty tends to write with a religious atmosphere rather than a spiritual sensibility, but it is hard to ignore the man walking on the water in this song. It should be mentioned here that Tom Fogerty claimed this song as his own, which explains the difference. In a letter to John written in the 1980s, he says that he got the idea from The Animals' 'House of the Rising Sun' and Them's 'Mystic Eyes' and was seeking to reclaim the publishing for it. It is the only song credited to the two brothers on any Creedence album. They played it during their residency at Dino and Carlo's and occasionally in the period after the album was released. It is the definition of a 'deep cut' and is a real gem on this album.

Other Songs associated with Creedence Clearwater Revival
'Before You Accuse Me' (Bo Diddley)
As we will see, there are precious few out-takes or alternative versions available from this band. This was a fully realised effort that was left off the album at the last minute. John Fogerty wasn't happy with it and, in his memoir, refers to it as the 'Jefferson Airplane version'. It does involve a lot more chord changes than Bo Diddley used in the original (or in his entire career!), but it is a lot better than 'Get Down Woman'. Compared to the version on *Cosmo's Factory*, it is quicker and much more garage sounding. They had been playing this song since The Blue Velvets period and the concept to update here is like 'Suzie Q'. Fogerty sings it righteously and knocks out a couple of killer guitar solos. What's not to like?

'Call It Pretending' (John Fogerty)
This was the flipside of the 'Porterville' single and was never seriously considered for inclusion on the album. Fogerty felt that it was too much in a style they had left behind. I covered it in the previous section. It was the last non-album B-side they would ever do and is not a bad song at all.

Bayou Country (1969)

Personnel:
Doug Clifford: drums
Stu Cook: bass
Tom Fogerty: rhythm guitar
John Fogerty: guitar, voice, harmonica, keys
Recorded: October 1968, RCA Studios, Hollywood
Released: January 1969
Label: Fantasy
Producer: John Fogerty
Engineer: Hank McGill
Running Time: 33:48
Highest Chart Position: US 7, UK 62

An enduring idea about Creedence Clearwater Revival is that there is something remarkable about a kid from El Cerrito, California, writing songs set in the American south. With *Bayou Country*, John Fogerty begins to populate the imaginative landscape that will define his writing and the band. Bayou queens, people on the river, and narrators who pump a lot of something down in New Orleans or run around the woods on the fourth of July. For more than half a century, reviewers and profilers of the band have pointed out that these songs are not drawn from Fogerty's personal experience and that he had never been south of the Mason Dixon (not entirely true) when he wrote 'Proud Mary'. Mention Creedence to a group of music fans and someone will say, 'those guys aren't even from the south.' A million articles about the band lead with this observation. They are all missing the point.

Only a Northerner could have written 'Proud Mary'. John Fogerty is not a journalist or a historian, he is a storyteller. The south he is writing about was invented by northerners. It is the 'other' America, a mysterious and ancient place filled with fantastical characters and mythical landscapes. Even when southerners write about it, they employ the same tropes. Dr John's New Orleans, Howlin' Wolf's Mississippi and Tony Joe White's Louisiana are only some of the examples of southerners mythologising their home. When Lynyrd Skynyrd, a band from Florida, attempted to explain the south in less mythical terms, they were dropped into a box called 'Southern Rock', which soon developed its own confederate flag-draped mythology.

It's not a question of authenticity. John Fogerty has never claimed to be more than another storyteller fascinated by the exotic quality of the American south. Robbie Robertson, who grew up further away in a whole other country, based his songs on the stories told to him by his drummer, Arkansas native Levon Helm. But it would be naïve to think that 'The Weight', 'The Night They Drove Old Dixie Down', or 'The WS Walcott Medicine Show' are any different in terms of a realistic depiction of life in the south than John Fogerty's 'Proud Mary'. Edward Said, who famously wrote about Orientalism or the way that the

'East' is mythologised in the west, always insisted that it was primarily a system by which the idea of the 'orient' was perpetuated by writers, academics, and artists. The point to keep in mind is that John Fogerty didn't invent this idea of the south any more than Robbie Robertson did. Both were drawing from ideas that went back at least 150 years in stories, songs, plays, and paintings. It is significant that John Fogerty begins his memoir by reminding readers that Stephen Foster, the 19th-century writer of such songs as 'Oh Susannah', 'Camptown Races', and 'Swanee River', was, in fact, from Pittsburgh.

For John Fogerty, some of the drift into a mythic landscape was the result of sitting in front of the television in 1968. It was, even by our contemporary standards, an eventful year throughout the world. Protests in France, Czechoslovakia, Northern Ireland, Brazil, Japan, and a lot of other places created a sense that the whole world was up in arms. Closer to home, the protests in Chicago during the Democratic Party convention that summer would have been impossible to ignore. Earlier, there were the assassinations of Martin Luther King – an event followed by widespread rioting and social unrest – and Robert Kennedy, the leading Democrat in the 1968 primaries. American involvement in the Vietnam War was also escalating in the wake of the TET Offensive, which began in January of that year, something that must have felt close to home to the recently discharged John Fogerty. He has commented that *Bayou Country* was a themed album about the south and that Robert Kennedy's death played some role. The South, then, is not only an imagined landscape but a nostalgic one. There is a long history of rural life representing something essential and pure to the urban dwellers. Fogerty uses the example of Stephen Foster's 'Swanee River', sometimes known as 'The Old Folks At Home'. Leaving aside the more questionable lyrics, it is all about a longing for a place in Florida that had locals scratching their heads over the location. This southern fantasy is now their state song.

Creedence was now in the unenviable position of following up their first taste of success with 'Suzie Q'. John Fogerty's mantra at the time amounted to 'I'm not going back to working at the carwash fellas' while he taught himself to write hit songs. They were still playing at Dino and Carlo's at the beginning of the year but were also doing shows at venues like the Avalon Ballroom throughout 1968. They were playing with bands like Blue Cheer, It's A Beautiful Day, Steppenwolf, and Ace of Cups at these shows before returning to their regular Tuesday night gig at Dino and Carlo's in North Beach. They were beginning to play gigs further afield, but Creedence remained a Bay Area act. I can imagine John Fogerty sizing up bands like Steppenwolf or Blue Cheer and asking, 'what can I do to get above the pack?' Both of those bands would enjoy a degree of success – Steppenwolf in particular – and both were part of the second wave of 1960s bands. Blue Cheer's proto-metal garage-psych and Steppenwolf's no-bullshit V Twin rock were both appealing, but Creedence were simply too rooted in rockabilly and 50s R&B to be able to do loud 'acid rock', as it was sometimes known at the time, convincingly It was up to John

Fogerty to find another way into the late 1960s rock and roll scene.

The album was recorded at RCA studios in Los Angeles. There was a fair bit of fairy dust on the console as the Rolling Stones had come up with the hit version of '(I Can't Get No) Satisfaction' here in 1965 and returned the following year to record the masterpiece that is the *Aftermath* LP. The list of hit singles and albums recorded here in that period is a long one so Fogerty must have had to push hard at Fantasy to record there in October 1968. It certainly paid off. The engineer they worked with was called Hank McGill and credit must be given to him for helping Fogerty realise his sonic ambitions.

'Born on the Bayou' (John Fogerty)

John Fogerty has regularly said that this song grew out of a soundcheck jam at the Avalon Ballroom. It's not entirely clear what show he is referring to, but they did play a benefit for the striking employees of KMPX FM in March of 1968, a few months before 'Suzie Q' became their first hit. They were at the bottom of the bill and thus had to soundcheck last. During the check, John began to play around with the E7 chord played in a C7 shape up the neck. He shouted at Stu to 'play in E!' and started wailing nonsense sounds over the PA. It was sounding great when it all stopped. They'd been unplugged and the sound guy told them it was time to finish. 'Let's face it', said the weary crew member, 'you're not going anywhere anyway.' It was an unpleasant comment, but it did not deter John Fogerty. 'Give us a year', he retorted. In a year, they could no longer play venues as small as the Avalon.

Focusing on the main riff, this is the point to mention Roebuck 'Pop' Staples, the patriarch and guitarist for The Staples Singers, a gospel act who came to incorporate folk, blues, gospel, and soul in a long and fascinating journey. On the Staples' early recordings for Vee Jay records, one of the distinctive elements (aside from Mavis Staples' angelic voice) is Pop's blues-soaked vibrato-laden Fender Jazzmaster. My reaction, upon first hearing their 1956 recording 'Uncloudy Day', was 'hey, that sounds like John Fogerty!' He has acknowledged the influence of gospel generally and Pops' guitar work over the years in interviews.

Not discouraged by the cranky Avalon sound guy, the band continued to develop the song during their Tuesday night residency at Dino and Carlo's. The lyrics, according to Fogerty, came from the imaginative idea of the 'South' that he had absorbed from the lyrics of his favourite blues artists – Howlin' Wolf, Muddy Waters, Bo Diddley – and two films that he has mentioned over the years.

The Defiant Ones, a 1958 late-period noir, directed by Stanley Kramer and starring Sydney Poitier and Tony Curtis, is an interesting choice. The plot involves two men, one African American, the other White, escaping from a chain gang. They are, of course, chained together and though it does not start off well, their relationship develops as the film goes on. It is meant to suggest something about the nature of interracial politics in the south at the time and is a film of the civil rights era. John Fogerty was inspired not by the social commentary but the depiction of the landscape. It was shot in lavish black and white and won the Oscar for best cinematography that year. The fact that it fed John Fogerty's imaginative sense of the south is fitting because the outdoor scenes were filmed in California. As we will see, Fogerty's 'South' is tied up with childhood memories of rural California, so this makes sense in a roundabout way.

The other one happens to be French director Jean Renoir's first effort in Hollywood, a 1941 film called *Swamp Water* that starred Walter Brennan, Walter Huston, Anne Baxter and Dana Andrews. It's a standard, though somewhat dense, noir-style story of a fugitive appearing in a small town but it is best known for a quicksand scene towards the end. This time, John Fogerty's interest in the landscape is better placed as the outdoor scenes were filmed on location in the Okefenokee Swamp region of Georgia. The chase scene through the swamp must have inspired aspects of the song. John Fogerty has referred to himself as an 'American sponge' which isn't a bad description of a song that combines Hollywood films with Pop Staples' guitar work.

With *Bayou Country*, the band established an approach to recording whereby they rehearsed the songs intensively in their practice space at a warehouse in Berkeley. When they went into the studio, all that was left was to record them. Bands of the time did something like this to avoid exorbitant studio fees, but John Fogerty's regime was more austere than others. The lack of outtakes available would suggest that the decisions about arrangements and which songs were to be included were made before anyone pressed the record button. Various band members have noted that the songs were usually done in three or four takes with minimal overdubs. Anyone after a lost gem would be advised to check the air around Berkeley, as that is where those outtakes exist today. Little was left to chance. John Fogerty knew what songs would be released as singles and made sure that these were worked up to perfection.

'Born on the Bayou' is heavy on groove. Nobody is showing off. The guitar solo sits within the perimeters of the song and Stu's bass part is melodic enough to keep things fresh in the slow tempo. Tom Fogerty's light touch on rhythm guitar is on show here too. If this song had been on the first album, it could have been stretched out, but there is no need. It sounds like a long song, but it isn't. At under four minutes, it doesn't outstay its welcome and every second is precious. Even at Woodstock, where anything would have sounded brief after two hours of the Grateful Dead, they keep it under five minutes.

The lyrics don't tell a story so much as create an atmosphere to go with the groove. Not for the last (or, with 'Porterville' in mind, the first) time, Fogerty writes from the point of view of a character who has left a particular setting and now remembers it through a series of images. The father, like the one in 'Porterville', has struggled with authority and warns his son about the dangers of 'the man.' The 'man' was, of course, a byword for authority in the 1960s. An intriguing detail comes in the second verse, where the narrator remembers running through the backwoods on, of all days, the fourth of July. This detail suggests a deeper dream of freedom in an American Eden of open spaces in which to move. The verse ends with the narrator's dog 'chasing down a hoodoo there'. The word 'hoodoo' can mean any number of things from syncretic Caribbean religious practices to bad luck. In this case, it is the latter. The combination of the fourth of July with hoodoo is an early example, in John Fogerty's lyrics, of what critic Greil Marcus famously called, 'The old weird America', a setting far removed from the corndogs and baseball advertising imagery of the early 20th century. Not surprisingly, this song makes an appearance in his book on the matter, *Invisible Republic: The World of Bob Dylan's Basement Tapes* (1997).

In the next verse, the narrator wishes they were back on the bayou, 'rollin with some Cajun queen'. The Cajun people are synonymous with the bayous of Louisiana. 'Cajun' is a corruption of Acadian, which is the old name for an area encompassing sections of the Canadian provinces of Nova Scotia, New Brunswick, Prince Edward Island, along with the Gaspe Peninsula. After the French defeat on the Plains of Abraham at Quebec City in 1763, the French citizens of Acadia – already in trouble for refusing to sign an oath of allegiance to the British crown after the area was taken by the British in 1710 – were expelled and made their way to the remaining French territories of North America, including Louisiana. Some ended up in the Spanish territories too.

Rollin' makes an appearance here as it will more famously in 'Proud Mary' along with John Fogerty's Shakespeare moment with the word 'chooglin''. I will deal more thoroughly with 'choogle' soon. 'Born on the Bayou' is a song beloved of both band members and fans alike. It is with this song, the first track of *Bayou Country*, that Fogerty's vision, of which there are glimpses as far back as the mid 1960s, comes into focus. The unmistakeable opening riff is the starting point for Creedence's imperial phase and their annus mirabilis of 1969.

'Bootleg' (John Fogerty)

The groove continues with 'Bootleg', a meditation on the joys of forbidden fruit. At the time, the word was not widely used to refer to the sale of illegal recordings, although it was first used in this context in 1929. The first real rock bootleg, *Great White Wonder*, a collection of unreleased Bob Dylan recordings, wouldn't appear until July of 1969. This bootleg is a reference to hiding illegal whiskey in one's boot during prohibition and the well-known fact that people drank a lot more during that period. The three verses give examples of how things that are free or legal aren't as appealing.

Tom Fogerty's guitar part underpins the song here. He is playing a Fender Kingman, which was an acoustic guitar with an electric pickup. As his younger brother says in his memoir, 'Tom had great rhythm, in the same way that Elvis did if you listen to those early records'. There is some idea that John overdubbed an acoustic guitar, but the fact is that Tom is rock solid on this track. John adds Hubert Sumlin-style blues riffs on his ES 175 to give the song a Howlin' Wolf feel. The mention of water in the first verse echoes Wolf's 'I Asked For Water (She Gave Me Gasoline)'.

It's not a major song but contributes to the overall fabric of *Bayou Country*. It shares something with 'Keep On Chooglin'' as a song designed for the stage. Fogerty was clear about the songs that were going to be singles, those that would be deep cuts on the albums, and those that would fly live. This stayed in the set throughout 1969, notably at Woodstock. On a 2016 covers compilation album called *Quiero Creedence*, Los Lobos puts in a faithful but beautifully rendered version of 'Bootleg'. They slow it down slightly and draw out the rhythm. It's well worth hearing.

'Graveyard Train' (John Fogerty)

When *Bayou Country* appeared, it was noted by a critic in Stereo Review who thought this was the best song on the record because the band isn't 'looking for a gimmick'. I don't know what he means exactly, but there is certainly nothing remotely gimmicky about this song which, at 8 minutes, constitutes about a quarter of the album.

Doug Clifford says that it is John's tribute to Howlin' Wolf. If 'Bootleg' refers to 'I Asked For Water', this is nearly a cover of the song, a 1956 single for the Wolf. Of course, Creedence gives it a rockabilly groove, but it is essentially the same idea, a single guitar riff punctuating a sinister tale.

The story is a mashup of a haunted Robert Johnson-style narrative and Roy Acuff's 'Wreck on the Highway'. Thirty people have lost their lives on the highway when Rosie crashes into a Greyhound bus at the crossroads. Greyhound buses and, of course, crossroads are part of Robert Johnson's repertoire, so Fogerty is adding the blues tradition to the southern vision of this record. 'In the midnight, hear me crying out her name' echoes Wolf's 'hear me crying' in 'Smokestack Lightning'. The appearance of the undertaker is not unusual in a blues song. Buddy Moss's 'Undertaker Blues' (1934) is an example. The emphasis on coffins in the song is another blues trope that goes back to Ida Cox's 1925 'Coffin Blues'. The song winds up with the narrator asking to be taken to the station because he is number 31 of the dead, a ghost story ending to a spooky song.

'Graveyard Train' was apparently never played live by Creedence and is not a particularly well-known song by the band. In 1983, the classic lineup of the legendary Australian band, Beasts of Bourbon, covered it in swamp punk glory on their magnificent debut album, *The Axeman's Jazz*. Like all great cover versions, it draws out something essential – the menace in this case – and builds the song from there. This is the time to note the influence of Creedence on the Beast of Bourbon's guitarist Kim Salmon whose Scientists had recorded the timeless 'Swampland' the previous year. Salmon has been noted as a key influence on the early Seattle 'grunge' bands. The long shadow of John Fogerty!

'Good Golly Miss Molly' (Robert Blackwell, John Marascalco)

If *Bayou Country* can be seen as something of a concept album, then the only cover on the album is worth considering. The choice of Little Richard's 'Good Golly Miss Molly' makes a statement, something like: 'we can rock hard but not like Jimi Hendrix. Our idea of hard rock is Little Richard'.

'Good Golly Miss Molly' was originally recorded in New Orleans by Hendrix's old bandleader in 1956 and featured legendary sidemen such as the saxophone deity Lee Allen and soon to be Wrecking Crew drummer Earl Palmer. It was released in 1958 on Specialty Records and was a major hit for the singer. The writing credit shows Little Richard's producer Otis 'Bumps' Blackwell and songwriter John Marascalco, but there is no doubt that Little Richard gave the song its shape. He borrows the opening of Jackie Brenston's 'Rocket 88', considered by some to be the first rock and roll song, before launching into a furious rhythm and blues rant complete with dramatic stops and a killer sax solo from Lee Allen.

The lyrics are standard fare. Miss Molly loves to ball – ahem, dance, as in balling the jack – and rock and roll. She does this day and night at the house of blue lights; an establishment celebrated in another rhythm and blues standard by that name. Some have suggested that this is a reference to a brothel but is probably closer to the sort of disreputable establishments where Little Richard had learnt his trade as a performer. To tame this wild woman, Little Richard decides to buy her a diamond ring. There are, as with his other hit, 'Tutti Frutti', plenty of theories about what this all means, but it is all in the delivery which, in this case, is nothing short of fabulous.

The song has been covered many times, of course, and it likely went back to The Blue Velvets days for this band. It was in the set list when Saul Zaentz came to see them play and offered them a contract. Mitch Ryder and the Detroit Wheels' 1966 'Devil With A Blue Dress'/'Good Golly Miss Molly' single surely appealed to the band. Like John Fogerty, Ryder was an old-school rocker with no interest in lysergic ruminations. His last hits with the Detroit Wheels, 'Sock It To Me Baby' and a version of The Marvelettes 'Too Many Fish In The Sea' in 1967 anticipated the classicist direction taken by Creedence the following year on their first album.

All of this said, Creedence's version is solid but not a major moment on the album. Without a piano at hand, the song is based around a simple guitar riff and some nifty lead work from John Fogerty. He handles the vocals well and knocks out a couple of great solos. Otherwise, it has the feel of a song that they have played live to the point of boredom.

It is entirely competent and helps to build the atmosphere on the album but lacks the fire that they will later display on their rewrite of the song, 'Travelin' Band'.

The band played a partly lip-synched version when they appeared on the Ed Sullivan show in March of 1969, but it didn't feature regularly in their set lists after 1968.

'Penthouse Pauper' (John Fogerty)

Possibly the least known track on *Bayou Country* is this Albert King-style twelve-bar blues. The lyrics are in the 'if I was a...' folk style but are also out of the bragging tradition associated with the 'twelves' in pre-war blues. 'If I was jewellery, I'd be a diamond ring'. 'If I was a gambler, I'd never lose'. The punch line is that the speaker has nothing and is a 'penthouse pauper,' poor with big dreams. 'When you got nothing, it's all the same' is in line with Fogerty's working-class view of the American dream.

John Fogerty doesn't mention this song by name in his 2015 memoir, 'Fortunate Son', but he does mention his admiration for Albert King's 1967 *Born Under A Bad Sign* album that featured the guitarist backed by Booker T and the MGs. He says that it was a band favourite. 'Penthouse Pauper' channels songs like the title track and 'The Hunter'. John Fogerty's blues playing here is solid if unexceptional. In some ways, he was figuring out what sort of guitar player he was on *Bayou Country*. There is no question that he had some blues chops, but it was the rockabilly element that would come to define his style.

'Penthouse Pauper' does not appear on any surviving CCR setlists and has not been widely covered by other bands. Southern rockers Molly Hatchet tackled it in 1980 on their *Beatin' The Odds* LP. They rock it up and it is better than you think!

'Proud Mary' (John Fogerty)

Some songs sound like summer. 'Proud Mary' remains Creedence Clearwater Revival's best-loved song. It's an optimistic statement about following your heart and avoiding the 9 to 5 drudgery. The last day of school, the beginning of a long journey, a renewed sense of freedom, John Fogerty packed a lot into 3 minutes and 7 seconds.

The song emerged in the weeks after he received his military discharge papers. Creedence's music was famously popular with soldiers in Vietnam and one can imagine them relishing the song's promise of a life beyond the discipline of the military and the dangers of a warzone. Oddly enough, the titular Mary in the song began as a cleaning lady before an episode of the *Maverick* television show inspired Fogerty to turn her into a stern-wheeler river boat. But the dream of escape from the drudgery of working-class life remains in the lyrics as the narrator 'pumps a lot of 'pane' down in New Orleans. I should note here that there is some discussion of whether he means pain, as in a lot of suffering, or propane. Some have suggested that at a gas station, he would have cleaned a lot of window panes. Anyone want to run with a waiter pumping a lot of cham 'pagne' into rich people's glasses? I didn't think so.

The line about never seeing the good side of a city is important. The fact that the river represents an escape from class divisions echoes the way Jim and Huck transcend racial lines on their raft in Mark Twain's *Huckleberry Finn*. As with the bayou – which is a swampy river – this is a place where the original American dream of freedom and equality remains. It is another version of Fogerty's American Eden. The corrupting influence of money is absent here, too, as 'people on the river are happy to give'. This is an update of the old standard 'Big Rock Candy Mountain' where 'they hung the jerk who invented work'.

'Proud Mary' doesn't sound like the rest of the record. The other songs are blues-oriented, but Fogerty knew he had something with this one. When it became a hit – it reached number two on the Billboard charts, held off the top spot by Sly's 'Everyday People' and Tommy Roe's 'Dizzy' – it changed the sound of the band. The opening riff is, according to Fogerty, Beethoven's Fifth, but it is also a distant cousin to the opening of Wilson Pickett's 'Midnight Hour'. Fogerty's enthusiasm for Stax is obvious in the Steve Cropper-style rhythm guitar work. His love of male gospel groups like the Swan Silvertones inspired the 'rollin' rollin'' part of the song. And there is still something of a rockabilly rumble discernible here, particularly in the verses. Gospel, soul, and old-school rock and roll – John Fogerty had found his sonic lane.

Speaking of the male singers on this song, there is only one. John Fogerty was not happy with the backing vocals of his band during the recording sessions and told them so. A situation which had already begun to develop over the amount of input each member had in the band was exacerbated by this incident. Tom, Stu, and Doug went off to a San Francisco Italian restaurant called Two Guys From Italy and John recorded the backing vocals as a one-man Soul Stirrers. However, no one should feel as though they didn't contribute to this song. Doug Clifford's drumming is one of the key elements. A live version from a 1971 show at the Oakland Coliseum makes this case well. You can watch it on YouTube.

The song appeared during a particularly divisive period in America. The country's involvement in the Vietnam War split the country in a manner that continues to shape discourse there. People talked about 'heads vs straights' 'hip vs square' 'hawks vs doves' along with more obvious dichotomies like 'longhairs vs shorthairs' and, significantly in this period, 'old vs young.' The American dream was being questioned openly in the media and over tense Thanksgiving dinners throughout the country. An appealing quality of 'Proud Mary' was its benign nostalgia. It wasn't the dream of a 1950s America where 'values counted' and everyone loved the flag. This was, as in 'Born on the Bayou', a nostalgia for a much older America.

The Mississippi itself sustained the Indigenous people of the region for thousands of years before European settlement, before helping to realise the earliest American dreams. It is a key component of the geography of the US and facilitated the entire American project by providing irrigation and transportation. 'Proud Mary' is about the riverboat, but it is also about the river.

The riverboat is an important nostalgic element in the song. The paddle steamers that made their way up and down the Mississippi River are ingrained in the American memory. Mark Twain uses the image of a wrecked steamer to symbolise the end of the romantic south in *Huckleberry Finn*. He calls it the Walter Scott. Twain, whose real name was Samuel Clemens, was himself a riverboat pilot. He wrote about his experiences in *Life on the Mississippi*. John Fogerty has repeatedly noted his love for Twain's work in interviews over the years. The first modern musical, *Showboat*, was about life on a paddle steamer and Buster Keaton's famous film, *Steamboat Bill Jr*, uses the setting to comic effect. The figure of the riverboat gambler was made famous by the already noted 1960s television show, *Maverick*, but was also the subject of a Tyrone Power film called *The Mississippi Gambler* (1953). Paddle steamers remain a popular attraction at the various Disney theme parks.

Like the river itself, the boats represent a range of ideas, including commerce and mobility, while at the same time having an appealingly seedy aspect to their reputation. Gambling, prostitution, and smuggling were part of the world of the riverboat and, in the early twentieth century, the boats were one of the staging grounds for the rise of jazz music. No less than Louis Armstrong himself played on the boats in his early career.

The point of all of this is that John Fogerty had pulled off the considerable trick of writing a song that, if it didn't quite bring people together, it didn't divide them. There is nothing conservative or reactionary about 'Proud Mary'. The main character's story is essentially American. Tom Joad, Sal Paradise, Holden Caulfield, Billy The Kid. They all head out in search of adventure and freedom. Combined with an arrangement that was pop without being saccharine and fun without being vapid, this was, in some sense, the perfect song for 1969. From the father driving home from work to his teenage daughter doing her homework with the radio on to a young marine at the edge of the DMZ, it sounded like home.

It appeared in every live show the band ever did after it was released. There are hundreds of recorded covers and there probably hasn't been ten minutes since it was released that it wasn't being played by some bar band somewhere in the world. John Fogerty, in his memoir, recalls a hunting trip in the arctic sometime in the '90s where he heard an Inuit rock and roll band storm through it, unaware that its author was sitting in the audience. The most famous cover, of course, is Ike and Tina Turner's 1971 hit with the song. If I may offer an unpopular opinion, I think it sounds like every Ike and Tina shouter after 'Nutbush City Limits'. It's not terrible, but it doesn't bring anything new to the song other than what they brought to all of the songs they covered, i.e. Tina's voice, a powerhouse arrangement and something that got people out on the floor. I see articles where it is called the 'definitive version.' That isn't supportable. It is one of those covers that requires knowledge of the original and is, thus, just that, a cover. The Turners aside, most of the versions, including Leonard Nimoy's, are faithful to the original, suggesting that it is not only the lyrics that appeal to other acts but the whole package. Joe Dolan, Tompall Glaser, Solomon Burke, Tom Jones, George Jones, and Blitzen Trapper are a fraction of the artists who have tackled it but more or less stick with Fogerty's arrangement. Yes, Elvis' storming version is on his 1970 *On Stage* album. He recorded another live version a couple of years later.

John Fogerty says, 'it was the first good song I ever wrote.'

'Keep On Chooglin' (John Fogerty)

In case you are in Finland and want to request this song, Chooglin' in Finnish is Strumffatkaa. I know this because Finnish rocker and CCR superfan Kari Peitsamo recorded it in 1982. Presumably, 'Strumffatka' is a neologism in Finnish as Chooglin' is in English. John Fogerty has some catching up to do with Shakespeare, who supposedly coined new words numbering in the thousands, but he is off to a good start with this one. Chooglin' and its noun form 'Choogle' do not, sadly, appear in any dictionary, but surely it is only a matter of time. Fogerty modestly says that it was a fun word that incorporated shuffle and boogie, but it is not every musician who comes up with exactly the right word to describe an aspect of their music.

'Keep On Chooglin'' was created for the stage as the sort of boogie jam that was becoming popular with bands like Canned Heat. It's another long song that is not miles away from 'Bootleg' but has its own groove. There is a long harmonica solo from John, followed by a long guitar solo from John. The rest of the band choogle away agreeably while their leader shows his chops on both instruments. It must be said that few rock and roll musicians play the harmonica well. Most rely on one or two well-honed riffs, which, if they time them properly, can be effective. Fogerty is no Little Walter but produces a listenable if slightly chaotic effort here. His guitar solo is a different story. The Cropper influence, combined with his older rockabilly chops, brings this song to life. You can hear him shouting to the band when he begins a bar or two after the harmonica section. Gone are the occasionally leaden elements in his blues playing at the time. This is a lyrical and funky workout, ably aided by Stu Cook's lively bass work and Doug Clifford's solid time keeping.

The lyrics are blues doggerel where choogle could mean dancing or drinking or sex or all three. The band ended shows with this song, so there are many live versions to choose from, including several on film. They closed with it at Woodstock, but I would direct listeners to the version on *The Concert* live album. There is footage of this version too. The song has been covered only rarely, but Cajun accordion master Lee Benoit brings it all back home on his 2000 album, *Dis 'N' Dat*.

Other Songs Associated with Bayou Country

'Crazy Otto' (John Fogerty)

This is an instrumental recorded at the Fillmore West in March of 1969, around the time that 'Proud Mary' was catching fire. Crazy Otto was a car dealer who did late-night TV ads in the Bay Area at the time, but the song is better known to old-time Creedence heads as 'Blues Jam,' which is a pretty good description. John rips out another respectable long-form harmonica solo. He sounds a lot more competent on the instrument here than he does on 'Keep On Chooglin''. His guitar work is startling as always and the band are in great form behind him. Creedence outtakes are thin on the ground, so this is well worth hearing.

Green River (1969)

Personnel:
Doug Clifford: drums
Stu Cook: bass
Tom Fogerty: rhythm guitar
John Fogerty: guitar, voice, harmonica, keys
Recorded: March to June 1969 at Wally Heider Studios, San Francisco and RCA
Studios, Hollywood
Released: August 1969
Label: Fantasy
Producer: John Fogerty
Engineer: Russ Gary
Running Time: 29:25
Highest Chart Position: US 1, UK 20

Creedence Clearwater Revival recorded their first three albums for five
thousand dollars. In total! *Green River*, considered by many, including John
Fogerty, to be their finest moment, cost less than two grand to make over two
weeks. Recently, the world has been able to glimpse, in greater detail, the
making of what became The Beatles' final release, *Let It Be*. If anyone was in
doubt about how difficult it is to create an album before Peter Jackson's *Get
Back*, they should be clearer about it now. It is a long and frustrating process.
The documentary, of course, doesn't get anywhere near the mixing stage
either, which in the case of *Let It Be* was almost comically drawn out. No one
is claiming that 'Wrote A Song For Everyone' is as famous as 'The Long and
Winding Road', but it does remain a much-loved song more than half a century
later. Creedence put down the basic instrumental track in two hours. John
Fogerty returned to the studio the next day and laid down the vocal tracks.
After some overdubs here and there, he and engineer Russ Gary spent twenty
minutes or so mixing it.

I'm certainly not trying to claim that Creedence is somehow superior for their
work ethic or approach to recording but there is something remarkable about
John Fogerty's method. Wally Heider, whose brand new studio in San Francisco
was used to record the balance of the songs on the album, said that they were
the most efficient act he ever saw. They arrived with all the songs written,
rehearsed, and arranged. The three members who were not John Fogerty
complained about the regime, but their frontman was on one of the great rolls
in rock and nothing was going to stop him. The promise of a hit with 'Suzie
Q' had led to a much bigger hit with 'Proud Mary'. John Fogerty, who dreaded
being a one-hit-wonder, was determined to keep Creedence songs in the charts
and to feed the audience's appetite for his music before they were drawn away
by new confectionary. Where many musicians would have watched a single like
'Proud Mary' climb the charts and enjoyed their moment in the sun, Fogerty sat
down and wrote 'Bad Moon Rising'. While 'Proud Mary' was going gold in the

US, in between gigs and tours, he was making sure the band could nail his next hit in long, arduous rehearsals. It was released as a single in April of 1969, a few months before the album. The work shirt wasn't only a costume!

The band politics of Creedence is a complicated matter, but John Fogerty's artistic control was the source of increasing tension by the time *Green River* was recorded. Whatever was going on behind the scenes, the fact is that all the songs on *Green River* are, save for one, John Fogerty originals. This then begs the question of whether Creedence was simply a vehicle for one artist or was their music the product of a genuine group effort. Again, to reference Peter Jackson's *Get Back*, The Beatles moved slowly, but they were not, despite what has been written about this period, simply each other's backing group. The Beatles were a band that generally operated as such. The situation with Creedence is more complicated.

In the 1960s, film critics used the French word for author, auteur, to describe an approach to film criticism. Thus, a director like Alfred Hitchcock was seen as the principal creator of his films, despite the presence of actors, lighting directors, music composers, and all the other people who contributed to them. This approach drew from discussions of art or literature where work was considered as the product of the imagination of one painter or one writer. When popular music began to be treated more seriously by critics, they were faced with the same problem that early film critics found in writing about that medium. Who is responsible? The problem was solved by employing something like the 'auteur theory'. Early writing about The Beatles focused on the two principal songwriters. In the early to mid-sixties, critics would use 'Motown' as a stand-in for The Four Tops or The Supremes, or 'Phil Spector' as a way of discussing The Ronettes or any of his other productions.

My point is that Creedence Clearwater Revival was both a real band and the vehicle for John Fogerty's musical ideas. Regarding John Fogerty as the 'auteur' means that one can sidestep the argument over whether he simply was Creedence. In the way that Hitchcock alone did not make *The Birds*, John Fogerty did not alone make *Green River* or any of the remarkable records that followed. Tom Fogerty, Stu Cook, and Doug Clifford didn't write the songs on *Green River,* but they contributed through their playing and their understanding of John Fogerty's vision. John himself, despite years of ill-feeling and legal troubles, always makes it clear that what one hears on the records is a band interacting and responding.

So *Green River* is a contender for their best album. Fogerty took the basic elements of 'Proud Mary' and 'Born on the Bayou' and created a particular sound on *Green River*. The long blues jams are gone, replaced by nine songs, most of which are well under four minutes. He never showed much interest in the music of his contemporaries in San Francisco and, by the third album, is ignoring them altogether. Nothing on *Green River* sounds remotely like The Grateful Dead or The Jefferson Airplane. It was while touring to support this record that CCR played at Woodstock following the Dead, and, in Fogerty's recollection, waking up the crowd for Janis Joplin's pre-dawn set.

As noted above, the album was mainly recorded in San Francisco at Wally Heider's brand new studios. *Green River* was among the first albums recorded there after it opened in early 1969. It soon became one of the key recording houses in the world. There is no point trying to list the classic albums recorded there. Take out a few of your favourites from the period and chances are that at least one came to life in Wally Heider's.

Lastly, a note about John Fogerty's guitar situation. Early in the story of this album, someone helped themselves to the ES he had used on *Bayou Country* when he unwisely left it in the backseat of his Triumph outside of the studio on Hyde St in San Francisco. He scrambled around for a replacement and came up with a Les Paul Custom, which he used, along with a 1969 325 Rickenbacker, on *Green River*.

'Green River' (John Fogerty)

We've been on the bayou with Creedence and travelled the Mississippi on a riverboat. This album opens with another river and another nostalgic journey. Like the directors of the films that John Fogerty loved as a boy, the ones set in the south, he 'films' this story in California. He has said in interviews that he based this song on childhood memories of a vacation spot in the Putah Creek area near Winters, California, a rural town to the north of San Francisco. Tom Fogerty confirmed this in interviews, too. Cody, who is mentioned twice in the song, was supposedly the son of, or at least a relative of, Buffalo Bill Cody. The Fogerty family visited this place when John was four in 1949. It should be noted that his parents split up when he was young, so these vacations would be significant as a time when the family was together.

I mention that not to interrogate its Freudian implications but to highlight the extent to which this song, like 'Born on the Bayou' and 'Proud Mary', evokes a sense of a simpler time both in Fogerty's life and America in general. The nostalgia which permeates John Fogerty's songs and indeed the sound of Creedence is a key factor in their success. The extent to which CCR's music has been used in films, not only ones set in the period, suggests that there is an evocative element of memory in John Fogerty's songwriting. Another American writer comes to mind here. Ernest Hemingway's memories of family vacations in northern Michigan provide the setting for several of his 'Nick Adams' stories. In particular, 'Big Two-Hearted River' features Nick returning to a town in Michigan that has been destroyed by fire. He then seeks out the river where he goes fishing. The burnt village is considered by some to be a metaphor for the devastation of the first world war. Nick finds comfort in fishing for trout in the river. The river thus becomes a place of redemption or rebirth. This is an old metaphor. John The Baptist's ritual in the Jordan River is only one tradition that ascribes mystical healing properties to rivers.

'Take me back down where cool water flows, yeah/Let me remember things that I love' is how the song begins. Like the narrator in 'Born on the Bayou' who begins with 'When I was just a little boy…', this is a song about the past. As I have noted, part of the appeal of Creedence was, at least at this stage, that they were not singing about 1969, at least not directly. The songs acknowledge the appeal of better days. 'Old Cody, Junior took me over/said, "You're gonna find the world is smoulderin'/ And if you get lost come on home to Green River'. These are the final lines of the song. America in 1969 was smouldering, like Nick Adams' town in Michigan, but there was still a home in 'Green River'. This is another version of the American Eden. Considering that this is essentially a true story, it's notable that these lines are delivered by a relative of Buffalo Bill Cody, a fundamentally American cowboy figure who underlines the nostalgia of the song with his name. F. Scott Fitzgerald used the name for Jay Gatsby's early mentor, Dan Cody, 'a product of the Nevada silver fields, of the Yukon, of every rush for metal since seventy-five.'

In between are a series of images from the sensual – barefoot girls dancing in the moonlight – to those associated with childhood – rope swings, skipping stones. John Fogerty's America wasn't the one that owed Allen Ginsberg two dollars and twenty-seven cents or a place that Gary Snyder could almost love again. He is closer to Hemingway in this song. Fogerty's America was a summer of fishing, bullfrogs, and dragonflies. For a generation who barely recognised the place where they had grown up as it stood in the late '60s, there was something reassuring in Fogerty's lyrics. It wasn't reactionary or conservative; it was a dream of a lost childhood. The title of the song comes from the Green River Syrup used at the soda fountains of his youth.

A song this freighted with images and ideas needed music that would at once evoke earlier days but not turn it into 'Those Were The Days', Mary Hopkin's hit of the time. Part of Fogerty's program to keep the band in the charts and himself away from work at the car wash was to ensure that the band continued to evolve while somehow retaining the elements that their fans loved. With 'Green River', he attempted to create a 'bluesy rockabilly sound' that would have one foot in Sun Records circa 1955 and another in San Francisco in 1969. He wanted the guitar work to sound like one of his great heroes, James Burton, who, of course, created the memorable riff on the original 'Susie Q'. The Green River riff is an old Delta blues pattern that made the trip to Chicago after the war. Fogerty speeds it up into what one critic dubbed 'bluesabilly', a reasonable description of several CCR songs. Meanwhile, Stu Cook was recorded on electric bass before overdubbing a stand-up acoustic bass over the top of it. The acoustic bass was a mainstay of rockabilly but Cook doesn't play it in the percussive, snap-back rockabilly style of The Comets' Marshall Lytle or Elvis' Bill Black. Instead, he follows the more standard rock bass line that he has played on electric. Thus, the song balances Fogerty's retro guitar lines with a contemporary bass part. The effect is something akin to what the English critic Mark Fisher dubbed 'hauntological'. The word refers to the persistence of the past in the present and notions of 'temporal disjunction' where different pasts exist together in the present. It is, both lyrically and musically, a fascinating song and one of the highlights of this band's career.

'Green River' was a regular part of the live shows for the remainder of their career and was part of the setlist at Woodstock. The single, backed with 'Commotion', was in the charts in August of 1969 when the festival took place. It has been covered by a range of artists. Creedence fans, The Minutemen played it live on occasion and more recently, Eilen Jewell has recorded a lovely version. A cover worth hearing is M. Ward's 2006 release, where he deconstructs it in a thought-provoking manner. Of course, an act considered to be a formative grunge band was called Green River.

'Commotion' (John Fogerty)

'Commotion' was the B-side of 'Green River', their third number two single. This time, it was The Archies' eternal ear-serpent, 'Sugar Sugar', that robbed them of that elusive top spot. It's one of Creedence's great grooves, another of what John Fogerty refers to as his 'blues rockabilly' sound. 'Commotion' is more frantic than 'Green River' and Fogerty has said that he was trying to get a train sound. The repetition of the title with the 'co, co' stutter sounds like 'locomotion.' It's another great 'choogle' with a rockabilly-style descending bassline matching up with Doug Clifford's solid drumming. It was on this album that John Fogerty, along with engineer Russ Gary, worked out how to further enhance John Fogerty's vocals. By adding some echo, they found a way to favour to the rockabilly fabric of CCR's sound while at the same time giving John's voice the space it needed in the mix. His guitar work on this song is also notable and demonstrates his move away from straight blues toward his own unique blend of influences. Here, his James Burton instincts mix it up with Albert King for one of his strongest performances.

The lyrics, while not as rich as those of 'Green River', are still of interest. In 'Green River', Cody Junior warns him that 'the world is smouldering'. 'Commotion' describes that world. Fogerty has noted that there is a neo-Luddite strain in his work. There is a sense both in his music and lyrics that he is a man out of step with his time. 'Commotion' provides a glimpse of 1969 through John Fogerty's eyes. It's a noisy and confusing place where everyone is talking and everyone is in a rush. The first computers were connected through the Arpanet, an early version of the internet, in that same year. Fogerty was probably not aware of this development, but an increasingly frantic pace in American life must have been driving this technology. He mentions the need to save time in the song. Like others in his generation, he could recall a much less hectic world. 'Commotion' does not feature nostalgic images, but its subtext is a sense that life was better lived at a slower pace.

'Commotion' was played at Woodstock while the single was in the charts and it remained a feature of their live shows until the end. This song hasn't been covered as often as other CCR songs, but a few years ago, a cracker version by Uncle Tupelo appeared on a Record Store Day 45. The ever-reliable Kari Peitsamo recorded a Finnish language take in 1982. It must be heard for, if nothing else, the way he draws out the punk element of the song. In Finnish!

'Tombstone Shadow' (John Fogerty)

This is another twelve-bar blues track, inspired possibly by Albert King's legendary 1967 Stax album, *Born Under A Bad Sign*. The story is a blow-by-blow account of a visit that John Fogerty made to a fortune teller in San Bernadino (San 'Berdoo' in the song) in the early days of the band. In his memoir, he notes that he was told that he would have 13 months of bad luck and this came soon after he'd signed a contract with the man who would become his long-term bete noire, Saul Zaentz. Let's say that the fortune teller was out by at least 30 years. Also, in his memoir, Fogerty links it to 'Commotion' and his unease in the modern world. It's a provocative title in a series of death-haunted Creedence songs.

His approach to blues was changing by the time they recorded *Green River*. While he remains under the hoodoo spell of Howlin' Wolf, there is far more R&B in Tombstone Shadow than songs like 'Graveyard Train' from *Bayou Country*. He has abandoned the West Coast style 'blues jam' for a more uptown model. Southern Culture On The Skids recorded a version of this song with a country soul vibe that draws out the Stax influence.

'Wrote A Song For Everyone' (John Fogerty)

While listening to the *Green River* album, one tends to think, 'oh that one is on here too'. Keeping in mind that the era of LPs to simply capitalise on a successful single had only recently ended. The Beatles and Dylan threw up a challenge to the practice of recording 'filler' in the mid-1960s. *Green River* is a transitional album for CCR. Yes, it does include hit singles, but it also features superb album tracks. 'Wrote A Song For Everyone' is one of the band's best-loved songs, but it was recorded as part of the fabric of the album rather than as a chart climber.

John Fogerty came up with the idea for this song one Sunday afternoon in 1969. He was writing music, keen to keep up the momentum of his recent successes. His wife asked if he was going to be working all day and he nodded and kept strumming chords. She said she was going out and left. It occurred to the singer a few minutes later that he was trying desperately to communicate with his growing audience but couldn't spend an afternoon with his wife. John Fogerty didn't write confessional songs, as such, but he didn't avoid speaking from the heart. His memories, opinions, and relationships would continue to inform his songs for the remainder of the Creedence period and during his solo career.

But it is more than a 'my partner is miffed with me' song. The real tension in the lyrics is between the broader political or public world and the way we relate to the people in our lives. He has said that he was thinking of the politicians who could speak to their constituents but not their own kids as the generation gap widened in the late 1960s. While this is no doubt his memory of writing the song, the actual lyrics reveal a somewhat broader historical sweep with a reference to a recent news event at the time.

The first verse where the singer comes off the welfare line to go to war prefigures his observations in 'Fortunate Son'. The verses describe the wider world while the chorus repeats the paradox of writing a song for everyone except the person he needs to communicate with most. The wider world is, as Cody Junior points out in 'Green River', smouldering with injustice and danger. Richmond 'about to blow up' is likely a reference to a major news story in 1968 about a gas explosion on the main street of Richmond, Indiana that killed 41 people. The mention of people in chains and pharaohs evokes the sort of old-time spiritual that talked about slavery in coded references to the Old Testament. This is a verse about civil rights and the continuing inequality in the US. The politicians are the pharaohs spinning the truth. The song suggests that while these are all worthy topics, what the singer needs to do is talk to his wife. A broader moral might be that we need to help those closest to us before attempting to change the world. John Fogerty wasn't reactionary in any sense, but his politics are pragmatic and usually drawn from his observations rather than any ideology.

That said, this is a good time to mention that when a local Native American band occupied the Alcatraz Prison site near San Francisco, Creedence donated money to buy the leaders a boat. The occupation of Alcatraz was a radical move in a heated period of protests. Creedence's music was somewhat nostalgic, but they were never politically conservative.

John Fogerty refers to an earlier version of the song, which was recorded but subsequently erased. Like Shakespeare's 'ur Hamlet', we can only speculate on what it sounded like. I suspect it had a faster tempo, closer to 'Proud Mary'. He says that he wasn't happy with the drums, so it was re-recorded. The version that we have betrays, almost for the first time, his ear for a certain type of melancholy country song. Something in the world-weariness of the voice suggests Hank Williams.

There are many covers of this song out there. The most notable is Mavis Staples' version on the Jeff Tweedy-produced 2010 album, *You Are Not Alone*. Considering the influence that the Staples Singers had on CCR, it's worth hearing how she interprets one of John Fogerty's songs. Naturally, she excavates the soul gospel elements through her masterful delivery but sticks pretty much to Fogerty's melody and tempo. Jeff Tweedy covered CCR material in Uncle Tupelo and may have suggested this one to Mavis. There is a charming clip of the pair performing an acoustic version of the song on YouTube. If you aren't a great fan of this song, watch the clip and get back to me!

'Bad Moon Rising' (John Fogerty)

'Bad Moon Rising' has been dubbed the most cheerful-sounding song about the apocalypse. More cheerful than REM's 'The End of the World'? Or Prince's '1999'?

Or Nina's '99 Red Balloons'? John Fogerty has compared it to Guy Mitchell's 1956 'Singing The Blues', a song about a guy who has never felt so much like singing the blues but for some reason, is belting out an up-tempo pop tune.

This is one of the most covered Creedence songs. It has been done country, R&B, gospel, metal, punk, folk, bluegrass, and as a gentle ballad. It has been translated into German, Czech, Italian, Spanish, Greek, Danish, and of course, Finnish by Kari Peitsamo. It has been used in countless movies, including a famous sequence in 1981's *An American Werewolf In London*. The title was borrowed by Sonic Youth for their second album and the song has been adopted by soccer teams all over the world. It is also one of the most famous 'mondegreens' in rock and roll history, to the point that John Fogerty himself now sings 'There's a bathroom on the right' occasionally when he performs it onstage. It's also the case that people sing, 'Hope that you've got your 'shit' together' instead of 'things' these days.

It was another number two single for the band in the US, held off this time by Henry Mancini's 'Love Theme from Romeo and Juliet'. It spent three weeks at number one in the UK. The song, with 'Lodi' on the flipside, was recorded a few months before the album in February of 1969 and released in April of that year while they were making the rest of *Green River*. It proved that 'Proud Mary' wasn't a fluke and that John Fogerty was now part of a select group of songwriters who could make lightning strike more than once.

Like other Fogerty's songs, the inspiration came from an old film. This time it was *The Devil and Daniel Webster*, a 1941 adaptation of the 1936 short story by Stephen Vincent Benet, which appeared in the Saturday Evening Post. The story is a convoluted take on the Faust plot that pits the historical figure of Daniel Webster against the devil. Webster was Secretary of State to several presidents and a famous legal mind of the 19th century. In this 'only in America' retelling of the famous story, Webster defeats Satan, known in the film as Mr Scratch, and saves the soul of the character who earlier sold it to the devil for worldly success. It starred Walter Huston as Mr Scratch and Edward Arnold as Daniel Webster. John Fogerty found it spooky and was inspired to write 'Bad Moon Rising'.

Lyrically, it remains part of Cody Junior's smouldering world. Over the years, Fogerty has referred to the assassinations of Robert Kennedy and Martin Luther King as the basis for the grim atmosphere of his words. 'Don't come round tonight, it's bound to take your life', is a succinct summary of the mood in the US at the end of 1968. But 'Bad Moon Rising' now reads nothing short of prescient. The verses don't describe political or social turmoil, instead depicting the natural world in chaos. John Fogerty was evoking the wrath of God, Old Testament-style, but for today's listeners, 'hurricanes a blowing' and 'rivers overflowing' don't so much resemble the middle east 3000 years ago as the evening news. If only he'd added a verse about pandemics!

In about 1986, John Fogerty was at some sort of awards night when someone came up behind him and drawled, 'Give me back my licks!' It was Scotty

Moore, the genius who helped to invent rock and roll guitar with his inventive bebop-inflected playing on Elvis' Sun Sessions. Fogerty acknowledged that he had helped himself to Moore's licks regularly. As Charles Mingus noted, 'If Charlie Parker was a gunslinger, there'd be a whole lot of dead copycats'. Scotty Moore is more than another influence. His work is the basis for a lot of what followed in rock and roll. He had his own influences of course, including Merle Travis, Charlie Christian, and Django Reinhardt, but it was his playing that inspired the first generation of rock and roll players, who in turn inspired the next group. Fogerty has never made any secret of what he had in mind with the recording of 'Bad Moon Rising'. He wanted to recreate the Sun Records sound and, in particular, Moore's guitar work.

He pulls it off. By his own admission, it is a heavier beat, but the guitar work and the atmosphere recalls Elvis' 'I'm Left, You're Right, She's Gone', a 1955 recording released on the flipside of 'Baby Let's Play House'. The band sounds great with the rhythm section tight. They had begun playing rockabilly in junior high and this must have felt like a comfortable old black leather jacket for Stu and Doug.

This song, along with 'Lodi', was recorded at RCA Studios in Los Angeles in April around the same time that 'Proud Mary' was high in the charts and several months before the rest of the tracks on the record. John had, naturally, imagined the song on his ES, a rockabilly machine, but when it was stolen, had picked up a new Les Paul for the job. At the guitar shop, he plugged it into a Fender Twin amplifier and put the strings in Drop D – DADF#AD – tuning. He had his sound. The difference that the guitar and amplifier setup made to the song is made clear by the Woodstock version. Here, he is using his Rickenbacker and the song sounds much less rockabilly and far more garage punk.

As noted, there are many covers of this song. The Reels, an Australian band, scored a local hit with a slowed-down synthpop version in 1986. Jerry Lee Lewis recorded a snappy country version in a session in London in the early '70s that featured Albert Lee on guitar. Thea Gilmore's acoustic take from 2003 is worth hearing. It's one of those songs that is difficult to cover because the original is so convincing.

'Lodi' (John Fogerty)

The original *Rolling Stone* review of this record called this song, 'the true highlight' of Green River. It's a big call, but there is no question that 'Lodi' is one of the band's most affecting songs. It manages the difficult trick of perfectly matching the music to the story. 'Lodi' is about a particular musician and the song somehow sounds like the sort of song he might sing.

The town of Lodi, like 'Porterville', is in the San Joaquin Valley in California, although it is much closer to San Francisco. It was another town that John Fogerty chose for the sound of the name rather than for any personal connection. Fogerty claims that he had never visited Lodi when he wrote the song. The song is not a particularly good advertisement for the town, so he must have felt that karma was at work when, in the late '70s time of fuel shortages, he was stuck there in a mile-long lineup for a gas station. If you have seen the Paul Newman film *Cool Hand Luke*, and can recall the early scene where he is sawing off the top of parking meters, you will have seen Lodi's main street as it was in the 1960s. This section of the movie was filmed there.

The story is of a singer who comes into town to do one show and, for somewhat obscure reasons, never leaves. His career had been going well, but it has stalled and now he is playing to drunk and disinterested audiences. For Fogerty, who recognised, perhaps more than most of his contemporaries in rock and roll, how precious and rare it was to achieve success, the idea that it could all disappear in an instant resonates with him. There is something fantastical about the premise. The singer has been on tour, but somehow, his career has ended and now he is doomed to play the same lousy gig in the same lousy town for eternity. For touring musicians the world over, this song strummed a gloomy chord that they immediately recognised.

In a discussion of this song in his memoir, John Fogerty mentions the American novelist John Steinbeck. Something of the atmosphere of *The Grapes of Wrath* lingers in 'Lodi' with the Tom Joad-like character stuck in the wilds of California. There are different traditions in American literature and songwriting. For comparison's sake, many of John Fogerty's contemporaries wrote lyrics under the spell of the Beat writers of the 1950s. Bob Dylan, Jim Morrison, and Robert Hunter are only three examples. John Fogerty's models are much less esoteric. Names like Stephen Foster, Steinbeck, and Hank Williams crop up regularly in interviews. To paraphrase Bob Dylan's famous exchange with Mick Jagger, Bob could have written 'Lodi', but he would never have sung it. It is far too stark and revealing. Dylan's post-beat obfuscations are part of a tradition that draws from French movements like Symbolism and Surrealism. Fogerty is, in some measure, more American in his influences. He is more Thoreau than Rimbaud, more Hemingway than Breton. Dylan himself was, of course, the main influence on songwriters by this stage. Mostly everyone, even the all-powerful Beatles, had kissed the ring to some extent. But not John Fogerty. Creedence is one of a small coterie of 1960s American bands that somehow carried on as though Hank Williams remained the most important songwriter of the 20th century. That said, Bob Dylan proclaimed 'Proud Mary' his favourite song of 1968 and years later encouraged a reluctant John Fogerty to start singing it again.

'Lodi' has been covered by country artists, including Buck Owens, who would soon be namechecked in a CCR song. It is a natural fit but in some ways is more a song about country music than a country song itself. There is nothing self-consciously C&W about the arrangement or the instrumentation. Fogerty might have imagined himself writing in that genre, but the result is far too stamped with his signature sound. If you are shaking your head in disbelief, listen to Dan Penn's cover on his 1973 album, *Nobody's Fool*. The man who wrote 'Dark End of the Street', 'Do Right Woman' and 'I'm Your Puppet' recognises a soul song when he hears one. Fogerty is never far from Stax Records, not even when he is singing about a country singer out of luck in California.

'Cross Tie Walker' (John Fogerty)

This is one of the great 'deep cuts' in the Creedence catalogue, a classic train song hidden among the better-known tracks on this album. Keen-eared listeners will have noted that the titular character has already appeared on the album in the title song. The narrator of that song mentions spending his days with flat car riders and cross-tie walkers. This is the world of transient men riding the rails and living in the hobo jungles that used to spring up in the wastelands at the edge of cities and towns. Fogerty was old enough to have glimpsed something of this world before it disappeared, but, like Buffalo Bill Cody, these are characters from American myth cycles. He is tapping into Woody Guthrie's memoir, *Bound For Glory* and Jimmie Rodgers songs like 'Hobo Bill's Last Ride'.

The sound is one of Creedence's purest expressions of their love for rockabilly music. The 'train train' sequence is a homage to Elvis' 'Mystery Train', from his magical Sun sessions. If 'Bad Moon Rising' borrowed some of Scotty Moore's riffs, 'Cross Tie Walker' was glorious grand larceny. Doug Clifford knocks out a steady Fluke Holland rhythm while Stu Cook's descending bass punctuates the lines of the second verse before the first guitar solo. There are occasionally whispers that John Fogerty was let down by his rhythm section in Creedence. To those whisperers, I can only say, listen to 'Cross Tie Walker'. This is one of my favourite songs by the band and an excellent place to divine the powerful influence of rockabilly in the Creedence sound.

'Sinister Purpose' (John Fogerty)

'Sinister Purpose' picks up *The Devil and Daniel Webster* story that inspired 'Bad Moon Rising'. This time the singer takes the role of Mr Scratch, the Devil, and says that he will come to get you and that the roots of the earth will shake. The 'sinister purpose' of the title is the Faustian bargain: 'I can set you free/ Make you rich and wise/You can live forever/Look into my eyes'.

The highlights of the song are John Fogerty's 'sinister' guitar solos and fills. The on-beat rhyming couplets of the verses are hokey, but the chorus works well. It's not a major song, but it fits into the overarching theme of Cody Junior's smouldering world. Southern Culture On The Skids committed a rocking instrumental version to tape on their 1998 *Zombified* album. The Booker T/Ray Manzarek style organ might make John Fogerty wish he had done something similar. I think it works much better as an instrumental.

'The Night Time Is The Right Time' (Nappy Brown, Ozzie Cadena, Lew Herman)

There are a lot of night times that are also the right time. The original by Nappy Brown is a raw classic and it has been covered by, among others, Bobby Darin,

Lulu, Rockin Dopsie, Adam Faith, Etta James, The Animals, Aretha, The Mighty Diamonds, and The Sonics. The classic, however, is by Ray Charles. But which version? Brother Ray recorded a stunning studio take that reached number 5 on the R&B charts in 1959, and there is a sweet version on his classic *Live At Newport* album, which came out around the same time. John Fogerty, however, was partial to a less known rendition from a 1960 live album called *In Person*, which was recorded outside with a single microphone on, yes, a rainy night in Georgia.

Fogerty plays the famous opening sax section on electric guitar and the whole thing has a garage aspect – which is a good thing! It's one of those covers where the band manages to convey both deep respect for the original and the sheer joy of making it their own. Creedence's cover versions are highlights, but this exuberant take is particularly poignant at the end of what is arguably a gloomy LP.

Other Songs Associated with Green River
'Broken Spoke Shuffle' (John Fogerty)
John Fogerty is not keen on outtakes and extra tracks. He spent a lot of time planning the albums and feels that the additions to subsequent editions interfere with the integrity of the albums he painstakingly created. It's a valid argument. As fans, we want to hear everything, but some artists feel that their vision must be respected. The capacity of CDs meant that it was easy to include extra tracks and, of course, there was a marketing dimension to offer something like a 40th Anniversary Edition with new material. Creedence might have the least to offer in this line of any major band. Their 'deluxe CDs' depend mainly on live versions to pad out the offerings.

'Broken Spoke Shuffle' and 'Glory Be' were done as test tracks at Wally Heider Studios to determine if it was a place where they could make their next album. The studio was being finished when these tracks were made. This one is not miles away from 'Cotton Fields', which would appear on their next album. It's worth hearing and is a good way to discern some of the key elements in the Creedence sound. The interplay between Doug and Stu, Tom Fogerty's rock-solid rhythm guitar work and John's southern fried licks are all on show here. The band doesn't always get the credit it deserves for its influence on the emergence of Americana in the '90s. This is a good place to wonder why that is the case!

'Glory Be' (John Fogerty)
This is from the same session and is another showcase of the band cranking away like a well-cared-for V8 engine. This was a test session for the studio, but it would be a good test track for any young band. This is what 'tight' sounds like, kids.

Willie And The Poor Boys (1969)

Personnel:
Doug Clifford: drums
Stu Cook: bass
Tom Fogerty: rhythm guitar
John Fogerty: guitar, voice, harmonica, keys
Recorded: Fall 1969 at Wally Heider Studios
Released: November 1969
Label: Fantasy
Producer: John Fogerty
Engineer: Russ Gary
Running Time: 34:31
Chart: US 3, UK 10

Creedence was not the first, nor the last, band to invent a musical alter ego to frame an album. The Beatles' 1967 *Sgt Pepper's Lonely Hearts Club Band* and Frank Zappa's 1968 *Ruben and The Jets* are two famous examples from the same period. The name *Willie and The Poor Boys* was suggested to John Fogerty by AA Milne's character, Winnie The Pooh, but the idea runs much deeper on this album. If the 'concept' of *Green River* was Cody Junior's contention that the world was 'smouldering', *Willie And The Poor Boys* is concerned with class divisions in America. Class remains an awkward topic in a country that was supposed to have superseded all of that with the Enlightenment concept of 'equality'. The 'poor boys,' like the hapless singer in 'Lodi', are part of Fogerty's America, a place with haves and have-nots. Despite the nostalgia, his vision is not impeded by glasses of the rose-coloured variety. In his terms, America is a good place but could be better; the values are solid but only when they are remembered.

The sound of the album, as signified by the cover, is more stripped back on some songs. Instead of the obligatory soul cover, they go deep into that other American songbook, the folk one, for two songs that predate rock and roll. But the soul influence remains, as does the rockabilly overlay and the blues sensibility.

This was the third album from Creedence in their remarkable year of 1969.

Bookended by the first masterpiece of *Green River* and 1970's *Cosmo's Factory*, *Willie And The Poor Boys* sometimes struggles for attention despite having at least two of their most famous songs on it.

From the cover, shot at Oakland's Duck Kee Market, to the quirky title to the evergreen anger of 'Fortunate Son', this was one of the final albums of the 1960s and one of the most compelling. It is a Janus-faced record, combining a backward glance at the decade behind it with anticipation for the one coming up. It digs deep musically to what is fundamental in rock and roll in a different but not so different way to bands like The Stooges and The MC5. It looks around at America finishing off a tumultuous decade and asks what is important now.

It's also a great record to put on at a party to get people dancing.

The album was recorded following the end of the tour for *Green River* in late September and the release date of the album on November 3. 'Down on the Corner', backed with 'Fortunate Son', was released a week or so earlier in late October. As with the previous albums, the songs were rehearsed for a few weeks, then recorded quickly at Wally Heider with engineer Russ Gary. The process was not without hiccups, as we will see, but, by my reckoning, they couldn't have spent more than a month on this album, start to finish. Seeing as John would have had to teach the songs to the band and work out arrangements in this time, it is a remarkable achievement.

In the gear department, John continued to use his Rickenbacker and Les Paul on *Willie and The Poor Boys*. Stu Cook used a 1968 Fender Precision bass and, occasionally, a hand-painted 1965 Fender Jazz model. Doug Clifford used Ludwig drums up until *Green River* when he started using a Camco kit.

'Down on the Corner' (John Fogerty)

It's late October 1969 and you are listening to the radio. It's getting colder and one of the great summers of rock and roll, not to mention lunar exploration, is well and truly over. The sixties are coming to an end, even if the Vietnam war isn't, and, out in California, they are still looking for the person who murdered the actress and those other people. 'Sugar Sugar' is on the radio along with Elvis' 'Suspicious Minds' and The Temptations 'I Can't Get Next To You'. 'Green River' is slipping down the charts, but the DJ announces that he is going to play the new Creedence single. Not sure which is the A-Side; he plays 'Down on the Corner'. Suddenly it is summer again.

'Down on the Corner' is built around another irresistible riff that sounds, as some reviewers at the time noted, like calypso. Infectious is an overused word in music writing, but it applies here. It is a song that makes the listener smile. It sounds joyful and the joy, as with 'Proud Mary', is tied in with nostalgia and a simpler way of life. In songs like 'Green River' and 'Born on the Bayou', he creates a mythical landscape that incorporates aspects of Greil Marcus' Old Weird America alongside more mainstream images of days gone by – riverboats, tire swings, and fishing. Norman Rockwell, whose illustrations codified so much American mythology, depicted all three of those motifs in his work.

'Down on the Corner' describes the performance of a jug band. Jug bands appeared in the late 19th century in the southern US. They were primarily busking units that played everything from folk songs to early blues to ragtime to whatever anyone wanted to hear. The instruments were a mix of handmade items like the large jugs that played the role of tuba and wooden washboards for percussion. A string bass that used a wash pail to produce sound was another feature. Cheap instruments like kazoos and mass-produced guitars or banjos were part of things along with the German harmonicas, which had flooded the market around the time of the civil war. They operated in the cities along the Mississippi and some of the earliest jug band recordings were made in Memphis. Will Shade's Memphis Jug Band and Gus Cannon's Jug Stompers produced a series of remarkable recordings with several songs that will be familiar to fans of 1960s rock and roll. The jug bands disappeared during the Depression, but as a by-product of the folk revival, they became popular in the early 1960s. In 1963, The Rooftop Singers scored a hit with a song called 'Walk Right In' that Gus Cannon had played for nickels forty years earlier on Beale Street. Gus also wrote 'Viola Lee Blues', which was recorded by a San Francisco band that began its life as Mother McCree's Uptown Jug Champions before eventually becoming The Grateful Dead.

Creedence did not start as a jug band, of course, but there is something of *Willie and The Poor Boys* in Fogerty's story. Doug Clifford is Rooster on the washboard, Stu Cook is Blinky on the gut bass, Poor Boy is Tom on Kalamazoo, a cheap brand of guitars built by Gibson in the 30s and 40s. John is Willie, who plays harmonica and kazoo while dancing. The song, despite the jug band conceit, is a fantastical origin story of Creedence. As I mentioned above, the concept of 'class' pervades this album and the idea of a band playing for nickels is part of the fabric. By 1969, they had been together in roughly the same line-up for ten years. They were experiencing enormous success, but John Fogerty did not consider himself as a genius finally being recognised. His belief was that this was all the result of hard work and that any deviation from the process would result in the immediate end of their good fortune. 'Down on the Corner' is a happy song, but the sense that they were a band that played for nickels and could be that band again is the subtext here.

'It Came Out Of The Sky' (John Fogerty)

This track which was released as a single in Spain, Japan, Mexico and on an EP in Singapore, features the first appearance of Jody, who will turn up in 'Hey Tonight' and on John's solo song 'Almost Saturday Night'. John Fogerty has always said that he liked the sound of the name, but others have suggested that it is a tribute to Jody Reynolds, the rockabilly singer whose 'Endless Sleep' made such an impression on him. Here's my theory: It is a compressed version of the name John Fogerty. If you take out the middle seven letters of his name or simply say it quickly, you are left with something that sounds like Jody.

In this song, 'It Came Out Of The Sky', when he imagines a farmer in Moline, Indiana, falling off his tractor after something lands in his wheatfield, he is perhaps channelling his own good fortune and the hit songs that seem to be falling out of the sky. Jody is the little man who stands up to the government and the Vatican when they claim something that fell on his land. Even what sounds like a light and humorous song on the album is concerned with power. Nixon's vice president, Spiro Agnew, and Ronald Reagan (then governor of California) both make an appearance. Reagan is called 'Ronnie the popular,' a credible observation about the former actor's populist appeal at the time, but one that continues to colour American politics.

The lyrics were, again, inspired by cinema. John Fogerty grew up during the fifties, a golden age for science fiction movies. The combination of fear about nuclear weapons, rapid advances in technology, and the cold war created an appetite for films about hostile aliens like *Invaders From Mars* (1953) and ferocious monsters like *Creature from The Black Lagoon* (1954). The point in the song is that the 'it' that came out of the sky is never identified, but the title sounds like classic Saturday afternoon movie fare. Of course, John Fogerty, along with everyone else, had witnessed the moon landing earlier in the year.

John Fogerty has also mentioned another film in relation to this song. *Ace In The Hole* is a surprisingly relevant film from 1951 about a reporter who deliberately prolongs the rescue of a man trapped underground to revive his newspaper career. It stars Kirk Douglas doing his ruthless guy routine as the reporter. For its time, it is a surprisingly lacerating take on the moral corruption of news media, but it appealed to John Fogerty's worldview. The song mentions Walter Cronkite, the legendary CBS anchorman and Eric Sevareid, a famous war correspondent who appeared on Cronkite's show as a regular guest in the late '60s. The sense that Jody is being hustled out of his prize by the White House and the Vatican is compounded by his exploitation by the media. John Fogerty, who had rapidly become a celebrity, might have felt, as people in his situation often do, as though he had become public property. In the end, Jody says that the 'it' belongs to him, but he'll sell it for 17 million dollars. Ironically, John Fogerty would sell his 'it' – the songs – but spend decades claiming his recompense.

'It Came Out of The Sky' is a straight-ahead 1950s-style rock and roll song in the Chuck Berry mode. Unlike others who imitated the guitarist's songs, John Fogerty makes it his own with sharp rockabilly licks punctuating the lyrics. This is exactly the sort of 'choogle' that Stu and Doug specialise in, so this is high octane stuff. Tom's rhythm work provides the groove under the melody. It's not clear why it wasn't released in the US or UK markets as a single. It is not on the top shelf of their songs, but it is close and contains the magic formula of fun and kick-ass rock and roll that was popular with their fans. It was a reasonably regular part of their setlists until the end of the band in 1972. It has been covered here and there, but the highlight is a 1985 version by Australian punk legends, The Scientists. Leader Kim Salmon is sometimes called the 'father of Grunge' and his embrace of Creedence here is another link between Fogerty and Seattle.

'Cotton Fields' (Huddie Ledbetter)

The arrangement that Creedence employs on their version of Leadbelly's 1940 song was made famous by the folksinger Odetta and her early singing partner, Larry Mohr, on a 1954 live album recorded at the Tin Angel in North Beach, San Francisco. The album was released by Fantasy Records, so Creedence was bringing this one home. That said, John Fogerty's inspiration for their version comes from The Highwaymen (not the country supergroup), an early '60s folk group who recorded it in 1962. It's worth listening to their version to hear the influence that this sort of proto-folk-rock had on Creedence's sound. As Fogerty says, they were more Buddy Holly than folk. The song had been recorded by a lot of people by the time Creedence tackled it. Harry Belafonte's version was likely the best known to the casual listener.

The Beach Boys recorded and released not one but two versions of 'Cotton Fields' at about the same time as Creedence. The first appeared early in 1969 on the *20/20* LP and as a single in some markets, but not the US or UK. They then re-recorded and released it in 1970 in the US and UK.

Without putting too fine a point on it, this is another song about memory and another reference to labour. Leadbelly's lyrics are about a baby being rocked in the 'Cotton Fields' of Louisiana. This is one of two songs associated with the singer that Creedence recorded for this album. It would take a long time to tell Leadbelly's story, but his influence and importance to rock and roll cannot be overstated. The songs that he wrote and/or arranged form an alternative great American songbook. He is sometimes known as a blues singer, but his vast repertoire included gospel, ragtime, jazz, folk, cowboy songs, and so on. He wrote 'Rock Island Line', which was recorded by the English singer Lonnie Donegan in 1954, jumpstarting the skiffle craze in England. This gave rise to, among others, The Quarrymen, who became The Beatles. No Leadbelly, no Beatles, George Harrison said. His songs formed the basis of the folk revival, and along with Woody Guthrie and Pete Seeger was one of the key influences on that entire movement. No Leadbelly, no Bob Dylan either.

John Fogerty wasn't happy with Doug Clifford's drum work on the song, so he edited a section out of each backbeat before re-recording all of the vocals and acoustic guitar parts. In a moment of unpleasantness, he gathered up all the edits, put them in an envelope, and dropped them off at Clifford's house. Relationships in the band had been fraying since the recording of 'Proud Mary' and this wouldn't have helped matters.

'Poorboy Shuffle' (John Fogerty)
The only time this instrumental was played live, according to John Fogerty, was while they were shooting the photos for the cover of the album. It's a credible imitation of the sort of barebones recordings made in the 1930s of street musicians in the south. As John says, they wanted to prove that they could play the instruments that they were photographed with on the cover. They certainly passed the audition. None of the instruments is particularly easy to play. Doug gets the shuffle beat down on the washboard while Stu – with the toughest task – matches him on the string bass. Tom plays acoustic guitar and John provides a close approximation of pre-war blues harmonica styles. It's brief but works well as an interlude between 'Cotton Fields' and 'Feelin Blue'.

'Feelin' Blue' (John Fogerty)
This is generally noted as the swamp rocker on the album from the same aisle as 'Born on the Bayou', 'Green River', and 'Keep On Chooglin''. The lyrics are

as downbeat as the title suggests. It's raining, there's a rope hanging ominously in a tree, and everyone is happy except the singer. The words, while not banal, seem secondary to the groove here. It is a one chord, one riff, slow burn that is something of a grower on an album with other obvious highlights. It's a song that John Fogerty came up with in 1967 but couldn't crack until the sessions for *Willie And The Poor Boys*. If Doug's drumming wasn't up to Fogerty's standards on 'Cotton Fields', he redeemed himself on this song. The rhythm section sounds vast here, like a diesel engine. Tom's rhythm guitar adds to the wall of sound behind John's righteous vocals ('Well, look up yonder!') and lead guitar work.

If it is swamp rock, it's on its way out of the swamp and heading towards Memphis and the offices of Stax Records. Fogerty has said in interviews that as much as he respected The Beatles, for him, Booker T and the MGs were the great band of the era. Their work as backing musicians on Otis Redding's recordings would be enough to seal their reputation, but they played behind most of the major Stax artists and were hitmakers themselves with a series of timeless instrumentals. Unlike other instrumental rock and roll acts, they got beyond their first smash hit, 'Green Onions', and grew as musicians and as a band. In 1969, they had scored yet another hit with 'Time Is Tight', one of the great soul grooves. Fogerty seemed to hear something in the interplay between the rhythm section and the melody as played by Booker T Jones on their records. The MGs are an influence on CCR's 'swamp' sound and 'Feelin' Blue' is where it is obvious. Listen to their 1966 single 'Booker Loo'. They weren't the only California band in the top ten listening to Booker T and the MGs. A little combo from Venice Beach with a singer called Jim comes to mind.

'Fortunate Son' (John Fogerty)
Is there anything in rock and roll like the first 18 seconds of 'Fortunate Son'? It's nothing flashy, a simple set of riffs over the drums and bass, but somehow, it sounds like the countdown to an explosion. Think of it like the theme music that builds tension in a film before the actors appear. Then Fogerty growls, 'Some folks are born to wave the flag' lingering on 'born' long enough so that the listener knows that this isn't going to be a patriotic song. Then he sings, 'oooooh, they're red, white and blue', and you know this is being delivered with irony.

'Fortunate Son' is among the most visceral protest songs of the 1960s. It has been called the first punk song, a phrase that means everything and nothing but speaks here to the raw fury of the song's sentiments and sound. The original target of the song was David Eisenhower, the grandson of President Dwight D. Eisenhower and the husband of Richard Nixon's daughter Julie. They were married in 1968. It wasn't particularly personal from Fogerty's point of view, only a sense that David Eisenhower (for trivia fiends – Camp David was named after him by his grandfather) was the same age as the young men being sent to fight in Vietnam. Eisenhower served in the Naval Reserve but was never anywhere near southeast Asia. For Fogerty, who, along with Doug Clifford, came perilously close to active duty, it was all too obvious that the people like Nixon were putting other people's kids in great danger. He was, by no means, the first person to make this observation. Siegfried Sassoon, the English writer, best known for his poems about life in the World War One trenches opened his famous protest letter with, 'I am making this statement as an act of wilful defiance of military authority, because I believe that the War is being deliberately prolonged by those now have the power to end it. I am a soldier, convinced that I am acting on behalf of soldiers.' Many of the poems of his fellow soldier poets either hinted at or directly pointed to the irony of old men sending young men to die. This observation has a long history that goes back to ancient times.

Fogerty follows the birth of the 'patriotic' American with, 'when the band plays hail to the chief, they point the cannon at you.' 'Hail To The Chief' is the song played when the president appears on formal occasions and the idea of a ceremonial cannon being pointed at you suggests that there is something murderous about the conduct of the American government. It's a serious charge and when it becomes clear what he is suggesting – that rich kids don't go to war, the song becomes every bit as bilious and pointed as Bob Dylan's 'Masters of War' and as unambiguous as Pete Seeger's 'Waist Deep in the Big Muddy'.

The second verse cleverly employs the silver spoon trope to create the image of the rich at a banquet helping themselves to a lavish feast. Fogerty's observation that they cry poor when the taxman comes around is a telling link to their reluctance to join the war effort in real terms. Fogerty's charge is, on one level, obvious, but there is also subtlety here. He has said that he is a proud American and was never attracted to radical politics in the '60s. What he does in 'Fortunate Son' is suggest that it is David Eisenhower and the others of his class who are the subversives. They don't pay tax; they don't do their duty as soldiers. Their patriotism is phoney.

Thus, it was astonishing in 2016 to see Donald Trump arrive at stump speeches with this song blasting over the PA system. Whatever one's views on the man, he somehow sidestepped active duty in Vietnam and, by his own admission, has avoided paying tax at times. It would seem like an own goal to remind the crowd of these two items with such a well-known song.

Except that the song now signifies something entirely different. In 1994, a film starring Tom Hanks called *Forrest Gump* used the song at the beginning of a Vietnam War sequence where the titular character arrives for duty by helicopter. Helicopters with musical accompaniment were already a Vietnam war movie trope following the memorable use of Wagner in Francis Ford Coppola's 1979 film, *Apocalypse Now*. Donald Trump or his people recognised that whatever the lyrics said, the song was now associated with *Forrest Gump's* reception as an essentially conservative film and, at the same time, hinted that Trump was somehow a 'brave soldier'. John Fogerty tried to stop him from

61

using it. He said that Trump was the sort of person he had in mind when he wrote the song. It's a truism that works of art take on a life of their own when they are sent out in the world by their creator, but this is a striking example.

Of course, there is always the possibility that even politicians can recognise a kickass rock and roll song when they hear one. John Fogerty, in his memoir, mentions a conversation with Dave Grohl (he re-recorded the song with the Foo Fighters for his *Wrote A Song For Everyone* album in 2013) where he made the point that the hardest song to write is a straight-ahead rocker. They must be simple but not dumb, full of emotion but not overwrought, powerful but not ludicrous. It's not an easy trick. For every 'Jumping Jack Flash', there are a hundred 'Life In The Fast Lane's. 'Fortunate Son' uses two straightforward chord progressions, one for the verse, the other for the chorus, to build its propulsive groove. It's the old garage rock formula, but where the singer in songs like Them's 'Gloria' drops behind the beat like a sulky teenager refusing to be hurried, the vocals on 'Fortunate Son' sounds like a horse galloping towards home.

There are plenty of covers to listen to out there. Cat Power does a good job fitting it into her style on her *Dark End of The Street* album. U2's take can be heard on a Super Deluxe version of their 1991 *Achtung Baby* album. Not surprisingly, it was covered by several American punk bands. The Circle Jerks' cover opens up the hardcore possibilities of the song effectively. Bruce Springsteen calls John Fogerty the 'Hank Williams of our generation' before kicking into a version with the man himself. The clip on YouTube is well worth watching as it makes clear the effect Creedence's music generally has had on Bruce.

'Fortunate Son' is on the National Recording Registry at the Library of Congress for its cultural significance. Fogerty wasn't a millionaire's son, but he managed to create something historic with 'Fortunate Son'.

'Don't Look Now' (John Fogerty)

The rock critic Ellen Willis who wrote the thoughtful entry on Creedence in *The Rolling Stone Illustrated History of Rock and Roll* thought that John Fogerty's political songs neatly avoided the smug liberalism of his contemporaries. She said that his protest songs were less 'we want the world, and we want it now' and 'more like you and me on a bad day'. 'Don't Look Now' is a case in point, a protest song that asks a series of uncomfortable questions for middle-class protesters. As I have noted, class is a tricky topic in American political discourse, but Fogerty wades further and further in on *Willie and The Poor Boys*.

'Don't Look Now' is another rockabilly rave-up, this time in Johnny Cash's shunting yard. Cash's style of early rock and roll was characterised by a metronomic steam engine shuffle behind his stories of heartbreaking moments and backbreaking work. Stu and Doug execute this with great style and Tom's rhythm guitar adds to the percussive rockabilly wall. John

Fogerty adds a spare riff and his best Cash vocals. Years later, Fantasy created a compilation called *Creedence Country* as another way to repackage the band's music. It's a pleasant if somewhat mystifying compilation as the tracks, including this one, veer much closer to rockabilly than anything resembling the Nashville sound of the 1960s.

In his memoir, 'Fortunate Son', John Fogerty says that he was 'prodding my generation a bit' with this song. This time, however, the target wasn't David Eisenhower but the counterculture. The 'hippie dream' was okay, but who was going to make the shoes and mine the coal? Johnny Cash, whose political sensibilities were similar to Fogerty's, released a 'work' themed album in 1963 called *Blood Sweat and Tears* that reached back in various traditions to songs about labour. It wasn't overtly left-wing and none of the songs were about unions, but it was meant to honour the idea of physical labour in a period where it was becoming more remote to a population moving to the suburbs. Fogerty's song would have fit in well if it had been available. The critic Robert Christgau wrote that the song was 'meant to encapsulate the class system in two minutes and eight seconds.'

Unfortunately, Cash did not cover 'Don't Look Now', but there is a strange and loose version by CCR fanatics The Minutemen and a blues take by former Blaster, Dave Alvin. CCR did not play it often, but it does appear on the 1970 Oakland show that formed *The Concert* live album.

'Midnight Special' (Traditional, arranged by Huddie Ledbetter)

In keeping with the loose concept of songs about work and class, Creedence covered a song associated with Leadbelly but with lyrics stretching back to the 19th century. Poet and folklorist Carl Sandburg included it in his 1927 *Songbag* collection, offering the opinion that there is something suicidal in the lyrics. For a train light to shine on you, you would have to be standing on the tracks facing the oncoming train. It makes sense in real, if overly literal, terms. John Fogerty heard Pete Seeger play it at folk festivals in the late '50s, but I suspect that Paul Evans' jerky rockabilly hit version from 1960 would have had greater appeal for Fogerty. Evans begins in the same halting manner though his version has far less swamp gas than Creedence's when the band kicks in.

Creedence's version begins with Fogerty's guitar in full Pop Staples reverb mode. He strums each chord and lets the first verse unfold. Then Doug comes in and the band starts up, at first paying tribute to Leadbelly's loping rhythm on his version. When it changes, The Staples Singers' influence is clear, giving it a gospel feel with rockabilly flourishes. It's a top performance and one of the highlights of the record.

'Side O' The Road' (John Fogerty)

A palette-cleaning instrumental before things get heavy indeed on 'Effigy'. The band's love for Booker T and the MGs is on show here. John's lead guitar work is, in the year of the electric guitar, understated and more about the groove than showing off. This sounds like a studio jam that found its way onto the album. It was never played live and though it is not substantial enough to qualify as a deep cut, it is nonetheless a part of the fabric of *Willie and The Poor Boys*.

'Effigy' (John Fogerty)

Since the 1990s, the Red Hot organisation has released a series of compilation albums to raise money for, and awareness about, AIDS. The third, which was called *No Alternative* appeared in 1993 and featured the cream of 'alternative' bands at the time. One of the most poignant tracks was Uncle Tupelo's version of Creedence's 'Effigy'. The band, which would soon morph into Wilco and Son Volt and is now regarded as one starting point for 'alt-country', doesn't deviate wildly from the original, but they pour everything into it and in the context of the album, it is an extraordinary statement. I was surprised that Fogerty didn't mention it in his memoir. They took a great song and made it relevant in a completely different context. Not an easy trick!

Fogerty wrote it after seeing Nixon dismiss a group of protesters at the White House. It isn't entirely clear in the song whose 'Effigy' is on fire, but the suggestion is a nation in turmoil. The 'palace' lawn of the White House points to an out-of-touch leader who is no longer listening to his subjects. The mention of the 'silent majority' is significant. In the 1968 election, Nixon appealed to a group of Americans who normally voted Democrat but were not interested in the counterculture or Vietnam War protests. It worked well, and American politicians have been vying for this mysterious group's vote ever since. Fogerty notes that when they elect a president like Nixon, they aren't 'keeping quiet' anymore. The fire is spreading from the palace lawn to the countryside, and it is possible that the 'Effigy' burning is, in fact, America itself. The repeated question 'Who is burning?' is cleverly ambiguous. Who is on fire? Who's doing the burning? Does it matter? It is a downbeat way to close an album that begins with the joyous 'Down on the Corner' but highlights the divisions in America in 1969, some of which he has outlined on the preceding songs.

It doesn't sound like other Creedence songs. It's built around a simple progression that sounds the relative minor as a major chord adding the seventh note. It gives the song an appropriately off-balance feel as the odd chord rings out. Fogerty doubles his vocals to further the eerie effect. There have always been some questions about the rhythm section of this band and, as must be obvious now, I think they are underrated. Doug Clifford's drumming is a key feature of this one and a good place to hear what he can do on a mid-tempo song. Similarly, Stu Cook's bass work provides the perfect foil to Fogerty's slicing guitar solo.

'Effigy' is one of the great 'deep cuts' in the Creedence catalogue. It's become better known since Uncle Tupelo's cover but remains a treat for those who

Creedence Clearwater Revival. Out of the garage and into the swamp. Two publicity photos, taken in 1968 (top) and 1969 (bottom).

Left: An exhilarating snapshot of a band taking flight. The self-titled debut album from 1968. (*Fantasy Records*)

Right: A swamp rock epiphany. The back cover of self-titled debut LP. (*Fantasy Records*)

Left: The Italian version of Creedence's debut LP. (*America Records*)

Right: 'Chasing down a hoodoo there'. The remarkable Bayou Country album from 1969. (*Fantasy Records*)

Left: Birth of the Choogle. The back cover of *Bayou Country*, 1969. (*Fantasy Records*)

Right: Huckleberry Finn with an electric guitar. 'Proud Mary'/'Born On The Bayou' 45 French picture sleeve. (*Fantasy Records*)

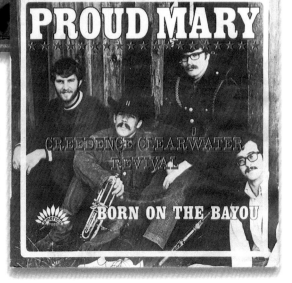

Left: John Fogerty's favourite Creedence album, *Green River*, in n1969. (*Fantasy Records*)

Right: Cody Junior's smouldering world. The back cover of *Green River*. (*Fantasy Records*)

Left: The apocalypse with a Sun Records overlay. One of CCR's most enduring songs is backed with one of their saddest. 'Bad Moon Rising'/'Lodi'. (*Fantasy Records*)

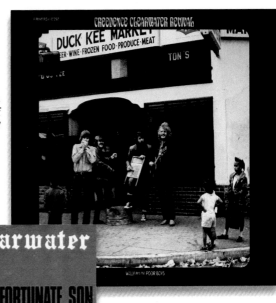

Right: This was one of the final albums of the 1960s and one of the most compelling. *Willie and The Poor Boys.* (*Fantasy Records*)

Left: Joy on one side, anger on the other. Double A side extraordinaire, 'Down On The Corner'/'Fortunate Son'. The Netherlands picture sleeve. (*Liberty Records*)

Right: Also a great record to put on at a party to get people dancing. Back cover of *Willie and The Poor Boys.* (*Fantasy Records*)

Left: John Fogerty on *The Ed Sullivan Show* in early 1969.

Right: The chemistry is obvious. Creedence on *The Ed Sullivan Show* in March 1969.

Left: Like the others in the rhythm section, Tom Fogerty used space rather than simply filling it. *The Ed Sullivan Show*, November 1969.

Right: Stu Cook and John Fogerty on *The Ed Sullivan Show* in March 1969.

Left: There are great drummers and there are great drummers who listen. Doug Clifford is the latter.

Right: It came out of El Cerrito. Creedence Clearwater Revival on *The Ed Sullivan Show*, March 1969.

Left: John Fogerty is a storyteller, a campfire orator. *The Ed Sullivan Show*, November 1969.

Right: Stu Cook is a smart bass player who finds his place in the arrangement. *The Ed Sullivan Show*, November 1969.

Left: Tom Fogerty took the rhythm part of rhythm guitar seriously. *The Ed Sullivan Show*, November 1969.

Right: Doug Clifford's timing, his ability to play rockabilly rhythms, and his poignant rolls, were all integral to the sound of the band. The *Ed Sullivan Show* in November 1969.

Left: They had been together for nearly ten years. Tom Fogerty and Stu Cook on *The Johnny Cash Show* in 1969.

Right: The fact that rockabilly rather than blues underpinned their sound is significant. *The Johnny Cash Show* in 1969.

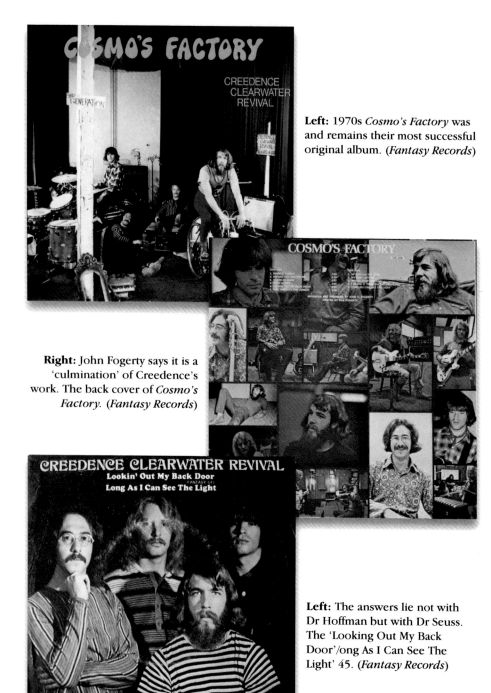

Left: 1970s *Cosmo's Factory* was and remains their most successful original album. (*Fantasy Records*)

Right: John Fogerty says it is a 'culmination' of Creedence's work. The back cover of *Cosmo's Factory*. (*Fantasy Records*)

Left: The answers lie not with Dr Hoffman but with Dr Seuss. The 'Looking Out My Back Door'/ong As I Can See The Light' 45. (*Fantasy Records*)

Right: It is, as they say, a grower. The *Pendulum* LP from 1971. (*Fantasy Records*)

Left: That difficult sixth album. The back cover of *Pendulum*. (*Fantasy Records*)

Right: It's a lot of people's favourite CCR song. 'Have You Ever Seen the Rain?' B/w 'Hey Tonight'. The German picture sleeve. (*Bellaphon/Fantasy*)

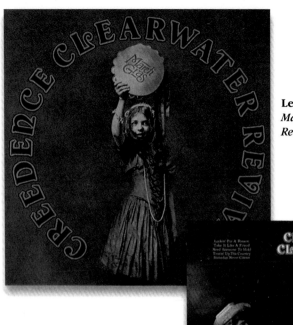

Left: The mystifying final album, *Mardi Gras*, in 1972. (*Fantasy Records*)

Right: The three-legged stool. Creedence without Tom Fogerty. The back cover of *Mardi Gras*. (*Fantasy Records*)

Left: As hitchhiking songs go, this is more Beach Boys than Doors. The 'Sweet Hitch-Hiker'/'Door To Door' German picture sleeve from 1971. (*Bellaphon/Fantasy*)

Right: Jack Bruce said, 'If Cream can play together, anyone can.' Except for CCR. A fraught evening at the Rock and Roll Hall of Fame in 1993.

Left: Doug Clifford at the Rock and Roll Hall of Fame Induction Ceremony 1993.

Right: Stu Cook at the Rock and Roll Hall of Fame Induction Ceremony 1993.

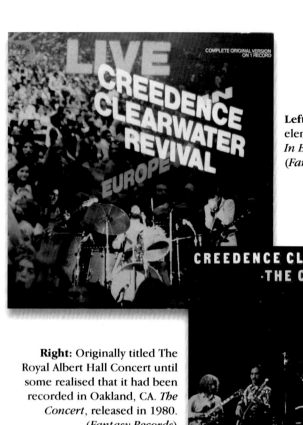

Left: There was always a 'garage' element in Creedence. *Live In Europe*, released in 1973. (*Fantasy Records*)

CREEDENCE CLEARWATER REVIVAL
-THE CONCERT-

Right: Originally titled The Royal Albert Hall Concert until some realised that it had been recorded in Oakland, CA. *The Concert*, released in 1980. (*Fantasy Records*)

Left: They had to wake everyone up after the Dead's set. Mission accomplished. *Live At Woodstock* released in 2019. (*Fantasy Records*)

Right: Recording of a *1971 Fillmore West* show. The sound quality is basic, but the band, now a trio, are on fire.

Left: One of the final live recordings of the original band with Tom Fogerty. *Boston Gardens 1971*.

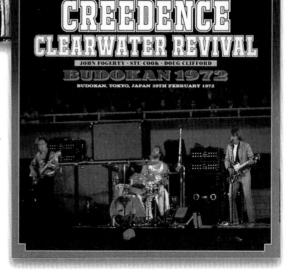

Right: An early show as a trio with all cylinders open. Budokan, *Tokyo Japan 1971*.

Left: A gift for Creedence fans. John Fogerty's second solo album from 1975. *John Fogerty.* (*Fantasy Records*)

Right: John Fogerty's comeback in the 1980s. A joyous album with some dark moments. *Centerfield* from 1985. (*Warner Bros*)

Left: John Fogerty comes to terms with the past. *Revival* from 2007. (*Fantasy Records*)

are mainly familiar with the hit singles. The band never played it live and John Fogerty has not revisited it in his solo career. It is a gloomy but compelling finish to one of the great rock and roll albums.

Cosmo's Factory

Personnel:
Doug Clifford: drums
Stu Cook: bass
Tom Fogerty: rhythm guitar
John Fogerty: guitar, voice, harmonica, keys, saxophone
Recorded: Late 1969 – 1970 at Wally Heider Studios, San Francisco
Released: July 1970
Label: Fantasy
Producer: John Fogerty
Engineer: Russ Gary
Running Time: 28:20
Highest Chart Position: US 1, UK 1

In Rolling Stone's original 1970 review of *Cosmo's Factory*, the writer sounded a cheerful note. "It's a damn good album by a group which is going to be around for a long time." About two years, as it turned out. But it is easy to understand why it seemed different to the reviewer. Creedence had come out of nowhere two years earlier and become the biggest band in America with a seemingly endless supply of hit singles and great albums. They were fronted by brothers and seemed like a happy team when they appeared on television. Their music wasn't hitched to psychedelia or any other overtly sixties style. If 'country rock' was the coming thing, as was sometimes suggested, their 'roots' sound would make them naturals. If confessional songwriting was on the horizon, then something like 'Wrote A Song For Everyone' was promising. Southern Rock, too, only a rumour at this stage, wasn't out of reach. They'd sort of accidentally invented it!

But clouds were gathering in the sunny skies over this classic summer band. The three members who were not John Fogerty were finding the one who was increasingly difficult. The name of this album sounds vaguely trippy but was a reference to the rehearsal space in Berkeley where the band would spend weeks on whichever next two songs were scheduled for release as 45s. By all accounts, the regime was punishing, and John Fogerty was an exacting leader. He recognised the fickle nature of rock and roll fans and was keenly aware that they were one dud song away from the top of a long slide back into obscurity. He wanted to put a new single in front of the public every three months and a new album every six. The first songs that would appear on *Cosmo's Factory* hit the shops less than two months after the release of *Willie And The Poor Boys*. 'Fortunate Son', on the way down, passed 'Travelin Band' on its way up to the top ten in early 1970. It's likely that there was a two-year period when there wasn't a CCR song somewhere in the charts in the US. This is astounding and explains how they outsold The Beatles and every other band in the world for a while but it took its toll. The rosy future with Creedence as contenders throughout the 1970s did not come to pass.

Too bad! A decade where Fogerty and co filled the space occupied by Messrs Frey and Henley is a lovely daydream.

Cosmo's Factory was and remains their most successful original album. It was number one in at least six different markets and, to date, has sold nearly twice as much as any of their other records. The reviews were better too. The 'underground' rock critics seemed to 'get' this one. Stu Cook and Doug Clifford have changed their minds over the years about their favourite albums, but both have regularly cited *Cosmo's Factory*. John Fogerty says that it is a 'culmination' of Creedence's work but prefers *Green River*.

I will be honest here. I don't think it holds together as well as the two albums that preceded it. Song by song, it is consistently excellent. All of the Fogerty originals are top shelf and the covers are well-chosen and executed with flair. My sense, however, is that it lacks cohesion. *Green River* and *Willie and the Poor Boys* were, in their own ways, concept albums that told a story. *Cosmo's Factory* is three singles and their B-sides, four covers, and 'Ramble Tamble'. It's a great collection of songs, but, as the kids ask Mr Natural, what does it all mean?

Oddly enough, if one was going to assign a concept to *Cosmo's Factory*, it would be one that would come to define the 1970s. It is an album that sees its principal writer, John Fogerty, turning inwards, not necessarily to himself but to the band. *Cosmo's Factory* is a Creedence album about Creedence. The cover, where the members are all pictured with treasured items, points in this direction. Cosmo was Doug Clifford's nickname and, John Fogerty was responding to the band's frustrations with the attention that he was beginning to receive as the leader of CCR. The cover, shot by another Fogerty brother Bob, includes a sign that says, '3rd Generation,' a reference to critic Ralph J. Gleason's suggestion that Creedence was a 'third-generation San Francisco band in the liner notes for their first album. Another sign says the name of the band followed by Beware of Dog with the final g hidden. On what might be a Lite Brite set on the floor in front of Tom are the words Neat Clean and Bluesy, a reasonable summation of the band's sound. The back cover is a series of photos of, yes, the band. The packaging draws attention to the band itself, which, though not a concept as such, does provide some context for the music contained within.

'Ramble Tamble' (John Fogerty)

This is Creedence's deepest deep cut, a song that was never released as a single and has never been playing in the scene of the film where the hero arrives in Danang. It opens the record and in the way that 'Green River' and 'Down on the Corner' set the stage for their respective albums, it is something of a mission statement for *Cosmo's Factory*.

It is one of those songs that strike the listener as an instrumental though there are indeed lyrics. They are themselves a series of images that sound like a summation of Fogerty's concerns. It's the 'smouldering' world where things are going wrong, and on top of everything, there is a mortgage to be paid.

There is also, curiously, an actor in the White House. It would be another ten years before a former Hollywood star moved in, but in 1970, Ronald Reagan's ambitions were no secret.

But the real power of 'Ramble Tamble' is in the sonic journey. It begins with about 17 seconds of a funky southern-style guitar joined bar by bar by the rest of the band. It's a classic CCR choogle until it shifts into a garage punk take on Scotty Moore's 'Mystery Train' riff from Elvis's Sun Records days. Guitars are layered until John Fogerty's familiar voice growls, 'Down the road I go.' At this point, it sounds like the heaviest, most punk rock thing the band has ever done until it morphs into a cosmic country instrumental section that sounds like the basis of 'Free Bird'. Indeed, a writer in Pitchfork thought it could replace the Lynyrd Skynyrd song as the greatest ever Southern Rock tune. Heresy! With a minute and a half left, it goes back to the psychobilly section and more vocals before the mystery train slows down and arrives at the station.

'Before You Accuse Me' (Bo Diddley)

This is a song that they recorded for their first album, but John Fogerty dismissed because he thought it sounded like Jefferson Airplane. As I mentioned in that section, it's in fact a stunning version that should have been at least used as a B-side. In any case, two years and four albums later, they attempted it again. It is worth going back and listening to the 1968 version because, alongside this one, it illustrates the degree to which Creedence found their sound in the intervening years. It's also much more faithful to the Bo Diddley original, minus the out-of-tune guitar, fortunately!

The original version appeared as the flipside to Bo's 'Hey Bossman' in 1958, in the middle of his initial hit-making phase. Its 12-bar blues simplicity and straightforward opening guitar lick made it a natural for 1960s garage bands like the 13th Floor Elevators, who played it live. It was part of their early live sets, which was how it came to be recorded for their first album. The fact that they chose to include it on this album supports the idea that *Cosmo's Factory* was something of a summation, or 'culmination' as Fogerty says, of their career so far. Bo Diddley is best known for his signature beat, but in the 1950s, he recorded all sorts of blues-oriented rock and roll tracks too for Chess Records. They were generally roughly recorded and raw. Bo's work is an important component of the CCR sound, so it is appropriate that they paid tribute to him on an album that includes several significant covers.

This version, unlike the 1968 take, opens with Bo's riff. The band honours the rough-hewn original here with a loping shuffle and jagged guitar interplay. John Fogerty keeps things appealingly simple. Stu Cook's bass work gives it a rockabilly feel and Fogerty follows suit with a guitar solo that leans closer to Eddie Cochran than Bo. It is sung with great confidence and grit by John Fogerty. Another comparison point is his voice on the 1968 version. It was recorded at the same time as 'Suzie Q', but he was still searching for his register then.

The band played it live in their residency at Dino and Carlo's but did not perform it on the tours that followed this album.

'Travelin' Band' (John Fogerty)

And speaking of early rock and roll stars, this sincere example of flattery ended up in court when the publishers who owned Little Richard's 'Good Golly Miss Molly' took issue. Considering that Little Richard knocked off Ike Turner's piano riff for the original, it seems ridiculous, but since John Lennon was successfully sued for the Berry-esque lyrics in 'Come Together' at about the same time, it was in the air. It was settled out of court, hopefully for not too much! There's no question that it is a tribute to Little Richard, but so is The Beatles' 'I'm Down'. John Fogerty had no luck in this area, as we will soon see with 'Run Through The Jungle'.

One of the features of the song is a saxophone part, played by John Fogerty. He wanted a Stax-style horn section but decided in the end to do it himself. It's okay, but one wonders what someone like Bobby Keys would have brought to this song. The Doors hired Curtis Amy for 'Touch Me', but John Fogerty did not enjoy employing studio musicians. In his memoir, he says that he thought there were too many horns (!) on the Blood Sweat and Tears album (presumably the second one) and he concludes that if you are paying sidemen, you want to get your money's worth. Creedence, at this point, was selling more records than The Beatles. They could afford a sax player. Fogerty says he likes the homemade feel of it. It sounds like Buddy Savitt on Chubby Checker's 'The Twist' as the song opens in classic style with a turnaround standing in for the descending 737 airplane.

There are a lot of songs about touring, most of them falling into the Bob Seger 'Turn The Page' box where the singer moans about how hard it is to be a rock and roll star. It's always occurred to me that those songs are a slap in the face to fans who would gladly change places. 'Travelin' Band' is brilliant because it makes touring sound exciting, which, compared to most people's lives, it is!

Doug Clifford is the secret hero on this one, his perfectly timed rolls punctuating the changes and working in with Stu Cook's rockabilly bass work. Fogerty plays a frantic guitar solo towards the end of the song that matches the furious tempo. It's not far off the pace of another tribute to air travel, The Ramones' 'I Want To Be Sedated'.

'Travelin' Band', backed with 'Who'll Stop The Rain', was released as a single in January of 1970, more than six months before the album appeared and hot on the heels of 'Fortunate Son', which remained in the charts. As usual, it was number two on the US charts, this time held at bay by Simon and Garfunkel's 'Bridge Over Troubled Water'. It's a natural live song, of course, and remained a regular feature of their sets for the next two years. It has been covered extensively. Bruce Springsteen has included it in his live shows off and on for years and Toronto blues legend Jeff Healey performed it with his band in the Patrick Swayze movie *Roadhouse*. Maybe the most affecting cover is by Bill Haley, who released it on the flip side of one of his final original singles in 1971. John Fogerty re-recorded it with Jerry Lee Lewis and others but never, regrettably, with Little Richard.

'Ooby Dooby' (Wade Moore and Dick Penner)

This is an important song. It was Roy Orbison's first hit. If he hadn't had a hit, he would have gone back to Odessa and become a geology teacher. Thousands of students would have benefited from Mr Orbison's guidance on igneous rock formations, but the world would have missed out on 'In Dreams', 'Blue Bayou', and 'Pretty Woman'. The influence of those early '60s sides is significant and it is difficult to imagine popular music without them. But it all started with 'Ooby Dooby', a song that was written by Wade Moore and Dick Penner, who had recorded as Wade and Dick for Sun Records. Their 'Bop Bop Baby' is a killer rockabilly song that must be heard. Wade Moore recorded 'Ooby Dooby' with a singer called Rod Barkely in 1955. Roy heard it and cut a demo with his band. He offered it to Columbia Records, who liked the song but not Roy. They gave it to Sid King and The Five Strings, who recorded a cool version. Roy then recorded it at Norman Petty's studio in New Mexico, where Buddy Holly would later record. It was released on a small Texas label. It impressed Sam Phillips, who signed Roy to Sun Records, where he recorded his third and best-known version. That's Roy himself on lead guitar.

Roy Orbison's early rockabilly work is generally ignored or seen as juvenilia alongside his hit-heavy phase at Monument Records. This is a shame because songs like 'Go Go Go' and 'Domino' are highlights of the Sun era and feature his badass guitar playing. John Fogerty's enthusiasm for lowdown rockabilly grooves is well documented and, with his extremely faithful cover of 'Ooby Dooby', he pays tribute to both an artist who inspired him and a component of the Creedence sound. It's one of those covers that says, why mess with perfection? The band know the song well and Doug Clifford shines here. Stu's re-creation of the original bass part is spot on and John updates Roy's guitar work only ever so slightly. The songs on *Cosmo's Factory* are, in general, played fast, and 'Ooby Dooby' is slightly quicker than Roy's original. Nowadays, when 'Ooby Dooby' has been covered so often and Sun Rockabilly songs, in general, are part of the wider culture, this choice seems too obvious. But in 1970, rockabilly music had yet to be revived formally. Blind Faith covered 'Well Alright' and Blue Cheer supercharged 'Summertime Blues', but bands like The Stray Cats were ten years away. To cover this song so faithfully at the beginning of a new decade was an important statement about Creedence's musical values.

'Looking Out My Back Door' (John Fogerty)

People used to say that Paul McCartney's insistence on multiple takes of 'Maxwell's Silver Hammer' meant that it was 'the song that broke up The Beatles.' John Fogerty doesn't exactly say that the recording of 'Looking Out

My Back Door' brought tensions to a head in Creedence, but it is certainly implied. Apparently, Tom was using the brighter pickup on his guitar after John had specifically asked him to use both pickups for a mellower sound. There isn't a lot of detail given, but Tom objected, saying that he could never hear himself on the recordings. This is a fair point. Tom is indeed not always easy to pick out of the mix. This was something of a beginning of the end for Tom in the band.

And it's such a cheerful song!

Speaking of The Beatles, did anyone believe John Lennon when he said that 'Lucy In The Sky With Diamonds' wasn't a drug song? I'm sure it was based on his son Julian's painting, but girls with kaleidoscope eyes and rocking horse people eating marshmallow pies sound more than mildly lysergic. Evidence would suggest that Lennon was not unfamiliar with the effects of acid and I'm sorry, but it sounds like a drug song to me.

So does 'Looking Out My Back Door' and lots of other people thought the same thing at the time, but, in this case, they were wrong. The singer's description of what is going on in his backyard certainly raises questions, but the answers lie not with Dr Hoffman but with Dr Seuss. In particular, Fogerty had in mind the children's author's first book, *And To Think I Saw It On Mulberry Street,* which appeared in 1937. The story is about a boy whose father tells him to keep his eyes open on his way to school but not to make up things. The boy sees a horse and cart, which evolves, in his imagination, into all sorts of fantastical versions of a drawn wagon. When he gets home, he tells his dad that he only saw a horse and cart. It's a whimsical story about the power of the imagination set alongside Seuss's signature illustrations. It remained a popular title until 2021 when it was withdrawn along with several other Seuss titles for content that was deemed racist.

The other source that Fogerty mentions in his memoir is a much less well-known children's book called *The House of a Hundred Windows* by Margaret Wise Brown. This was published in 1945 and it was a book he remembered from childhood. The story was about a cat who stays in the house to look out of all the 'windows' which are in fact, famous paintings. He says that his mother would read the book to him and then sing a South African folksong called 'Pretty Kitty'. Fogerty had a young son at the time, and like many people with young children, was probably revisiting his own memories of childhood. He had the idea of writing a children's song and that's exactly what he did. Despite the tantalising appearance of a flying spoon, 'Looking Out My Back Door' is as family-friendly as a Dr Seuss book.

The style is, in part, a tribute to the Bakersfield sound, a Californian response to the overly slick music coming out of Nashville in the 1960s. Its best-known proponent, Buck Owens, is mentioned in the song. Owens, whose 'Act Naturally' was recorded by The Beatles, is a far more important figure in the story of how country crept into late sixties rock and roll than is generally thought. For John Fogerty, there was the rough-hewn, rockabilly-influenced guitar work of Don Rich and Owens himself. The songs reached back to the honky tonk era of the '40s and '50s, along with some inspiration from Western Swing. Two words describe the sound best: Fender Telecaster. Though John did not generally use one, the twangy, stripped-back atmosphere is present in his work.

He uses a Dobro he'd picked up in Nashville for the distinctive opening riff and to colour the chorus. Doug and Stu knock out one of their trademark rockabilly rhythm combinations, something along the lines of Rick Nelson's 'Waiting In School'. It is, like so many songs on this album, done at a fast tempo.

The single went to number one in Canada, Australia, Norway, and Sweden. In the US, it was, as was becoming all too predictable, number two, this time held back by Diana Ross's version of 'Aint No Mountain High Enough'. It's been covered regularly, but the Stray Cats' version released in 1983 on the B-side of 'Rebels Rule' is worth hearing. They draw out the country elements in it effectively and it is a nice tribute from one generation of rockabilly revivalists to another.

'Run Through The Jungle' (John Fogerty)

This is one of Creedence Clearwater Revival's most compelling tracks and it remains one of the more haunting songs of the era. Of course, John Fogerty was literally haunted by it during the 1980s in one of the most bizarre plagiarism cases in rock and roll. People could hear the similarity between 'My Sweet Lord' and 'He's So Fine'. Others wonder why Leonard Cohen didn't go after Leo Sayer for 'When I Need You'. Rock and roll is full of 'homages' that skate pretty close to the line but in 1985, John Fogerty's single, 'The Old Man Down The Road' from the album *Centerfield*, came to the attention of the copyright owner on a song from 1970 that sounded way too close. The song was 'Run Through The Jungle' by CCR. In an 'only in the USA' moment, Saul Zaentz sued John Fogerty for stealing his own song. It took more than ten years to be settled, in Fogerty's favour.

After concluding that Fogerty's victory on the merits vindicated his right (and the right of others) to continue composing music in the distinctive 'Swamp Rock' style and genre and therefore furthered the purposes of the Copyright Act, the district court awarded Fogerty $1,347,519.15 in attorney's fees.

The right to compose music in the 'Swamp Rock' style and genre is now a legal precedent and part of the judicial history of the US. I have tried to avoid the complicated and ultimately tragic story of John Fogerty's decades-long battle with Saul Zaentz. It is well documented elsewhere. But, along with Neil Young being sued for not making 'representative music' by David Geffen, it is one of the more vindictive lawsuits in rock and roll. Fogerty took his guitar into court but unfortunately, no recordings are available. Now that would be a bootleg!

'Run Through The Jungle' was long believed to be about the Vietnam War. There is nothing specific in the lyrics but, since he had written 'Fortunate Son', it seemed like a natural next chapter. They told me 'don't go walking slow' sounded like the sort of instructions given to a young GI before a patrol 'in country'. 'Fill the land with smoke' and two hundred million loaded guns all sound like they come from the same landscape that Francis Ford Coppola would try to depict in *Apocalypse Now*. It has been used in several films to summon up the Vietnam War and many veterans felt that it accurately depicted their experience in South East Asia. According to John Fogerty, the song was not about Vietnam at all but America. The idea of the 'concrete jungle' had indeed been around since the phrase was used in the opening voiceover of the 1945 film *The Lost Weekend*. Fogerty maintains that the song is about gun violence in America's cities. I will give him the benefit of the doubt, but I still think that it sounds like a song about Vietnam. Song meanings do evolve in their creator's imagination, so I suppose he may have come to understand it as a song about gun control. Perhaps he felt uncomfortable about the first-person element. The Vietnam War remains extremely controversial in the US and the phenomenon of imposters claiming to be veterans remains a problem.

The opening is ominous. Using backwards tracked guitar sounds, they set the stage for what must be their darkest swamp rocker. Smoke, magic, mountains, and the suggestion not to 'look back' belted out over minor key riffs all make for a spooky song. The repetition of the title, followed by Fogerty's blues harmonica work, gives the song the sort of voodoo vibe that had been left off *Willie And The Poor Boys*. We are back in Cody Junior's smouldering world here. The band cooks on this track. Clifford, as I hope I am making clear, is underrated as a drummer. The basic tracks on CCR albums were recorded live on the floor. Clifford and Cook, song after song, build a groove that perfectly complements Fogerty's vision. To have been a fly on the wall the day that this was recorded!

It was released as the flipside of 'Up Around The Bend' in April of 1970 but is the better-known song these days. It has been covered a few times, but The Gun Club's 1982 version on their *Miami* album is the most convincing. If ever a band could add something to this song, it was this one. Jeffrey Lee Piece sounds possessed and avoids the banal souped-up 'punk cover' trap to deliver a restrained but updated take. I think it is the best cover of any Creedence song.

The phrase 'devils on the loose' comes from another CCR mondegreen. In a review of 'Down on the Corner', a writer heard 'doubles on kazoo' as 'devils on the loose'. Fogerty read the review and thought, 'yes, please!'

'Up Around The Bend' (John Fogerty)

This song, backed with 'Run Through The Jungle', was another Top 10 hit for the band in 1970. John Fogerty says that it was inspired by riding his motorcycle. The idea of travel as a metaphor for freedom is ancient and Fogerty puts it to good use in this song. Hank Williams' conviction that there is 'something over the hill I gotta see' is an ancestor of the appeal of what lies around the bend. The lyrics celebrate the open road with a series of images that are pleasant but don't, in a song about travel, ever seem to arrive exactly. It's been suggested that the 'sinking ship' is the band itself.

John Fogerty came up with it while fooling around with Marty Robbins' 1957 hit 'A White Sport Coat and a Pink Carnation.' He thinks now that he was playing it wrong and somehow found this song. The riff that opens it is one of Fogerty's deceptively simple masterpieces. As with the other songs he created with radio in mind, it draws the listener in and sets the mood. He has the knack of capturing the spirit of a summer afternoon without sacrificing depth. It's a difficult trick. There are plenty of great pop singles, but few work as well on the stage of a roadhouse as they do on a transistor radio at the beach. 'Up Around The Bend' is a good example of why Creedence was able to keep their music in the charts without 'selling out' or compromising their sound in any way.

The single reached Number 4 in the US charts and Number 3 in the UK, the best performing single across the Atlantic after 'Bad Moon Rising'.

'My Baby Left Me' (Arthur Crudup)
Arthur 'Big Boy' Crudup's original recording of this song is a top piece of evidence to present if you want to argue that rock and roll began well before Bill Haley or Elvis Presley. Crudup's 'That's Alright Mama' provided the eureka moment for Elvis at Sun in 1954. His cover of that song was his first commercial release. In April of 1956, his version of Crudup's 'My Baby Left Me' was released as the B-side of 'I Want You, I Need You, I Love You', his second single for RCA. The Crudup song was recorded back in January of that year, not long after Heartbreak Hotel so it retains much of his original rockabilly spark. The song was subsequently recorded by Wanda Jackson and nearly every other musician ever, but it is Elvis's version that had such a profound effect on the young John Fogerty. He remembers hearing it over the radio in a shop and thinking, 'that's what I want to do'. His admiration for Scotty Moore had already been made plain on the albums that precede *Cosmo's Factory,* but like 'Ooby Dooby', he decided to simply recreate the sound both as a tribute and to essay the contribution to the CCR sound made by records like 'My Baby Left Me'. Keeping in mind that this album is taking stock of the journey so far, it makes sense.

What grabs me about this version is the absolute fidelity to Elvis's recording. This is not Blue Cheer or The Who rampaging through 'Summertime Blues', or The Yardbirds hot wiring 'Train Kept A Rolling'. This is revivalism rather than iconoclastic reinvention. It would be a few years before a real rockabilly revival would take place and it would get started mainly in England, although American acts like Robert Gordon, The Blasters, and, of course, The Stray Cats would bring it home eventually. But no mainstream acts in the world of rock and roll in 1970 were doing what CCR did with this cover version. When the revival happened, Creedence's role in keeping the flame alive was rarely mentioned as they had, by that time, been consigned to 'dinosaur' status with their contemporaries. The Stray Cats were cool when they talked about Gene and Eddie. Citing CCR as an influence would have certainly raised eyebrows in 1981! That said, they did cover 'Looking Out My Back Door' as a B-side at the height of their career.

The band sounds great on this song, not surprisingly. Tom, Stu and Doug tie down the classic rockabilly rhythm while John provides the Scotty Moore parts and the vocals. Creedence was a band where everyone could play 'in the pocket' and 'My Baby Left Me' is an excellent illustration of how tight they were by this point.

'Who'll Stop The Rain' (John Fogerty)

The story was always that this song was inspired by the inclement weather at Woodstock. Eventually, this became a myth about John Fogerty somehow making up the song on the spot. He has acknowledged that he did write it in the weeks after the festival but despite the brown acid memories of some attendees to the contrary, it did not feature in their set.

It's one of Fogerty's more traditional protest songs, a folk-rock style ballad with a metaphor at the heart of the singalong chorus. The rain could be bombs falling in Southeast Asia, the tears of the poor, political rhetoric, or as contemporary singers have it, the weather associated with climate change. 'Clouds of mystery pouring confusion on the ground' could be something akin to Philip Larkin's arrow shower 'somewhere becoming rain,' a reflection on the random nature of life. It's one of Fogerty's sad songs that sound happy. He refers to the pointlessness of government initiatives and compares politics in Washington (Virginia is close to the capital) to the Tower of Babel. The word 'fable' is worth noting. Despite his nostalgia for a better time in America, by 1970, the dream was, by his reckoning, a fiction. This is the second song to suggest that Washington DC was a corrupt place. This is two years before the Watergate break-in and at least three years before people were aware of its implications. It is portrayed as the moment when America lost faith in their government, but Americans were becoming increasingly disillusioned throughout the sixties.

The final verse is about Woodstock, but it is a long way from the garden in Joni Mitchell's song about the festival. The image of the crowd trying to keep warm suggests a generation whose dreams are fading. Don McLean would soon tag the disastrous Altamont festival as a living hell in American Pie, but Fogerty isn't so sure about Woodstock. He sees real pathos in the crowd at Woodstock, the 'good' festival, desperate to keep dry in a downpour. It's a bittersweet memory of the famous event and unlike Joni, he was there.

This is not what the rest of the band specialised in, but it's a good recording. It's folk rock with a dash of country, a sound that would become popular in the first part of the decade to come. Artists like Bob Seger (who recorded a version with John Fogerty in 2013), The Eagles, Fleetwood Mac, and others would soon draw on Fogerty's model for acoustic-sounding songs that rocked. Tom's acoustic guitar playing is a feature of the song and both he and Stu sang backing vocals. John Fogerty was not keen on letting anyone else sing on the band's recordings, but he relented on 'Who'll Stop The Rain', the first time since 'Porterville' that the other members of the band were heard.

The band only performed the song once, apparently, and it was captured on *The Concert* live album. As the B-side of Travelin' Band, it reached 13 on the Billboard charts. It has subsequently become a frequent part of Bruce Springsteen's live repertoire, particularly if he is outdoors and it's raining. There are plenty of clips of him singing it and the crowd knows it well.

'I Heard It Through The Grapevine' (Norman Whitfield and Barrett Strong)

There are covers and then there is Creedence's audacious take on 'I Heard It Through The Grapevine'. It wasn't as though there was any shortage of excellent versions at the time. Gladys Knight and the Pips had reached the traditional CCR spot, Number 2, on the American pop charts (top spot on the R&B chart) with a version in 1967. It was written by Norman Whitfield and Barret Strong in 1966. Whitfield, a Motown producer, had the Isley Brothers or The Miracles in mind but eventually recorded a version with Marvin Gaye. Berry Gordy didn't like the sound of Gaye's voice on the track (go figure!) and it was not released as a single. Meanwhile, Motown was feeling the heat as Aretha's powerhouse version of Otis' 'Respect' pushed aside everything in its path to number one. Gladys Knight and the Pips' version is one of the early examples of Motown moving out of the formula that had yielded their hits. It's recorded in a loose southern soul-style take and became the company's most successful release to date. The following year, Berry Gordy released Marvin's version as a single after the album track became popular with DJs. It was a hit in the summer of 1968 when CCR was having great success with 'Proud Mary'. John Fogerty's story is that he heard Gaye's version in a hippie shop in San Francisco. He was only hearing one channel, though, as the other speaker was elsewhere. Whatever he heard, it made him imagine something swampy with that riff. He thought something like 'what would Duane Eddy do with this song?' and came up with a bass guitar/bass drum-driven version that took the song down to its fundamental building blocks.

It's audacious because Gladys Knight's version is magnificent, and Marvin invests his version with the dark jealousy implied by the lyrics. Covering Motown songs could be tricky. Some people love Vanilla Fudge's 'You Keep Me Hanging On'. I'm not one of those people. Creedence could have made a mess of this song, but somehow, Fogerty was able to hear the connection with his own music and make something that worked. The lengthy guitar solos are a matter of taste, but he can establish, over 11 minutes, the power of the groove that drives all versions of this song. Doug Clifford's drumming shines on this track as he and Stu underpin the riff. His signature rolls work to great effect at the changes and throughout the solo. By the end, he and John Fogerty are in a zone together and the effect is magical.

'Long As I Can See The Light' (John Fogerty)

A recent cover version of this song is by Hiss Golden Messenger and is on a Christmas record released in time for the festive season of 2021. It sits alongside 'Joy To The World' and 'Silent Night' and others on the album. Is it possible that one day it will replace that Mariah Carey song as a holiday favourite? Probably not, but it speaks to the spiritual element and the emotional punch of the final song on *Cosmo's Factory*.

John Fogerty should have found a professional to play the sax solo. Let's get that out of the way. What was fun on 'Travelin Band' sounds amateur here. Someone fabulous like King Curtis would have knocked it out of the park. But we can forgive him because he more than makes up for it with his vocals. Critics have suggested that this is his best performance on any Creedence record. The lovely chord change before the title phrase allows him to push his singing in any number of directions. He takes every opportunity and if his vocals ever sounded forced or performative, they don't here. John Fogerty gives in to his desire for keyboards and the band keep it simple but solid behind him.

Like a few other songs on the album, the lyrics take up the idea of travel and restlessness. Fogerty has said that it is about his sense of himself as a loner who was having trouble with the idea of home at the time. Whatever the personal circumstances, what came out was a meditation on faith that could be romantic, familial, or spiritual. The light is a metaphor for God in most traditions and other singers have used it similarly, including Hank Williams, whose 'I Saw The Light' has become a gospel standard.

'Long As I Can See The Light 'was on the flipside of 'Looking Out My Back Door' and despite its obvious lighter-waving appeal, it was never performed live by the band. At the end of a somewhat glum record, it sounded a hopeful note. Unfortunately, things were about to become much more complicated for Creedence Clearwater Revival.

Pendulum (1970)

Personnel:
Doug Clifford: drums
Stu Cook: bass
Tom Fogerty: rhythm guitar
John Fogerty: guitar, voice, harmonica, keys, saxophone
Recorded: November 1970 at Wally Heider Studios
Released: December 1970
Label: Fantasy
Producer: John Fogerty
Engineer: Russ Gary
Running Time: 40:58
Charts: US 5, UK 8

Ah, that difficult sixth album.

They only made seven. There are the two stunners, *Green River* and *Willie And The Poor Boys*. There is the classic *Cosmo's Factory*. *Bayou Country* establishes their sound in great style. The first album is uncertain but is raw and fabulous on tracks like Suzie Q and Porterville. *Mardi Gras* is a mediocre and disappointing final album that I will cover in the next chapter. That leaves their penultimate studio album, *Pendulum*. Some critics have declared *Pendulum* a 'neglected masterpiece' while others call it 'the beginning of the end for a once-great band.' John Landau, in the original Rolling Stone review, thought it was 'stiff' and that they should have stuck to making great singles. Superfan and critic Ellen Willis says that she liked the album, but it 'made her uneasy.' For the surviving members of the band, the music is secondary to their memories of a period in which Creedence was imploding. John Fogerty called *Cosmo's Factory* the culmination of the band's work so far. He doesn't say it in so many words in his memoir, but it's clear that he considers *Pendulum* a failure. He had something in mind that he couldn't realise. More about this later.

And then Tom quit. The album was finished, but the older Fogerty brother was tired of it all. He walked out of both the band and his brother's life. This wasn't a snap decision. If he left sometime early in 1971, then it must have been on his mind in November of 1970 while they were making the album. One thing you can say confidently about *Pendulum* is that the chemistry is different.

John Fogerty has said that he was exhausted when it came to make this record. It was their sixth album in three years. He had written all the originals, arranged all the covers, produced the albums, and toured endlessly. Before they made *Pendulum*, the rest of the band had insisted that he include them more actively in the making of the records. He says that The Beatles were the worst thing that ever happened to his band. Everyone wanted to write songs. Of course, as we have seen recently in Peter Jackson's *Get Back* film, it wasn't easy for even George Harrison to get his songs recorded. The nonplussed reaction to the song, 'All Things Must Pass', from Lennon and McCartney is an awkward moment in the documentary. It's not difficult to understand Tom, Stu, and Doug's frustration with John Fogerty. By his own admission, he was driven to create hits and had little time for the ideas of the others. Yet, listening carefully to the albums, all of them played a part in the success of the songs. Creedence is not only John Fogerty. Stu and Doug were a unique rhythm section and a key part of the sound. Tom was that rare rhythm guitar player who didn't showboat but took the rhythm part of the job seriously. There were rumours at one time that John had re-recorded a lot of the instruments himself on *Cosmo's Factory*. He squelches those stories in his memoir, noting that the basic tracks were recorded live on the floor and that this is what gave the music such vitality.

But the rest of the band demanded more say in things and John relented. He said that they could write songs and help with the production but only after the next album. It wasn't a trick, as we will see, but it bought him enough time to create *Pendulum*.

What did he have in mind? He'd had the hits and sold more records than The Beatles in 1969. They were the biggest band in America. *Cosmo's Factory* had sold something like five million copies. So why didn't John Fogerty use the same formula on *Pendulum*. He could have aimed for two double-sided singles. 'Have You Ever Seen The Rain?' B/w 'Hey Tonight' was one, but he could have sprinkled more fairy dust on 'Chameleon' and 'Born To Move' for another. He then might have cooked up another couple of rockabilly numbers, a soul cover, and thrown in a few other originals. *Pendulum* would have been another monster hit. The recipe was there, but he chose another path.

Rolling Stone magazine didn't love them. At the time, this was a problem in terms of credibility. *Rolling Stone's* decisions about who was cool and who wasn't continue to inform our ideas about sixties rock and roll to some extent. And the magazine was fickle. The Doors were cool until they became popular, then they sucked. The Lovin' Spoonful always sucked despite being a much better band than a lot of the so-called 'underground' bands so loved by the magazine. Creedence wasn't badly reviewed, but they were treated with a certain condescension. This was the era of 'the album' and *Rolling Stone* writers never tired of the phrase 'singles band' for CCR. This bothered John Fogerty. He should have brushed it off. Jim Morrison said in an interview that The Doors had become the band critics – meaning primarily *Rolling Stone* – loved to hate. No one hated Creedence; they just didn't take them seriously enough. John Fogerty had the sort of sales and radio play that other bands would have killed for, but he wanted more than gold records.

Artists are always on extremely dangerous ground when their motive for creating art moves beyond the simple desire to make something that represents their vision. The moment that John Fogerty decided that he was going to make an album that would give them more credibility, he was already in trouble. Fortunately, *Pendulum* is not a disaster or a major misstep. It's different and it is flawed, but it is still a satisfying record. It is, as they say, a grower. Aside from the two most famous tracks, nothing might grab you immediately if you are not familiar with it. But there are plenty of deep cuts here and an opportunity to hear Creedence at their least commercial. I wrote the first draft of a novel once about a band that disagreed on everything except their love for *Pendulum*. I couldn't imagine anything more idiosyncratic!

But did it work? Did Creedence succeed in convincing Rolling Stone that they were every bit as deserving of the respect accorded to The Band? No. A misjudged media event to launch the album was a disaster that saw the band mocked by the very publications it had been trying to impress. The reviews were lukewarm, but the album made it into the top ten in both the US and the UK. The single went gold and the band kept going without their rhythm guitarist throughout 1971 before breaking up the following year. I will discuss *Mardi Gras* in the next chapter, but *Pendulum* is the final Creedence album with all of the original members.

'Pagan Baby' (John Fogerty)

John Fogerty attended Catholic institutions for at least part of his time in school. He remembered a tin in the classroom where they collected money for the 'pagan babies' of the world. Unfortunately, the lyrics don't interrogate the idea much or say anything. They sound improvised to me. Still, it's a great title and the song opens the album in classic CCR style with a long choogle built around a killer riff.

It's heavy, noisy, and it was all done in one take. John Fogerty taught it to the band, and it was recorded – all within an hour. On the previous albums, his approach had been long rehearsals followed by a week or two in the studio. If *Pendulum* has a different atmosphere from those albums, it may be because it was prepared from scratch in Wally Heider Studios. It took a month and must have cost more than all their other albums put together in studio fees alone. The effect is noticeable in several ways. The long rehearsals for the other albums meant that arrangements evolved naturally. Though the other band members complained that they had no input, surely by playing a song repeatedly, they were making subtle contributions. Critics have noted that *Pendulum* sounds forced at times. They usually attribute this to Fogerty's quest for credibility with the underground. I suspect it is more a case of songs not having the time to grow in rehearsal. 'Pagan Baby' is a good example. It sounds like the blueprint for one of the great choogles but is somehow unfinished. The slightly meandering section with no singing after the verses sounds like it was waiting for some lyrics or an instrumental shape. The song chugs along agreeably but doesn't seem to go anywhere.

That said, the band is in great form, particularly Stu, who is relishing the harder approach with a muscular bass part. Tom, too, seems ready for 1970s-style hard rock and Doug Clifford hits as decisively as always. John plays jagged lead and gives the vocals his best Wolf howl.

Some critics have suggested that the heavier aspect of this song was a response to the rise of hard rock bands like Led Zeppelin or Free. Fogerty has mentioned other bands in relation to this album that I will come to, but it is likely that he could hear some potential for CCR in this area. 'Pagan Baby' is underdone, but it would have been interesting to see how far the band would have gone in this direction if circumstances had been different.

'Sailor's Lament' (John Fogerty)

This is one of the odder songs in the Creedence catalogue. If the band was engaging with the emerging hard rock sound on the album opener, they seem to be going with a calypso vibe on this one. Caribbean music would become influential within a few years in the form of reggae, but calypso (or mento) had a moment in the mid to late '50s with songs like Harry Belafonte's 'Banana Boat Song' and the Christmas favourite 'Mary's Boy Child'. Creedence was no stranger to folk music, but this is their only foray into anything resembling 'world' music. It's not over the top – no steel drums – but it is there. Fogerty doesn't say much about it in his memoir other than to note that it is one of three Creedence songs to feature the other band members' vocals.

The story is about a sailor, yes, lamenting the loss of his money in a poker game with someone called Poormouth Henry. While he tells the story, the backing singers chant, 'Shame, it's a shame'. The story feels half-baked. The singer has lost his money to a cardsharp and it's a shame, but other than the fact that the deck contains eight aces, there is no real punchline to the tale. Compared to a song like 'Proud Mary' where Fogerty creates a distinct narrative voice and a rich landscape, this is thin.

Instrumentally, things are more interesting. The opening slyly echoes Sly and The Family Stone's 'Everyday People' with bass and keyboard. As it is a CCR track, the expectation is that John Fogerty's guitar will soon kick in. It never does. Stu keeps things going with bass in the pocket with Doug while Tom strums away. Eventually, John Fogerty's slightly flat saxophone appears against what sound like bongos and other percussion instruments.

Like more than a few of the songs on this album, it's a long way from the rockabilly-inflected choogles that one associates with Creedence. But it is by no means a disaster and is, in fact, one of the more memorable tracks on the record. As with 'Pagan Baby', you are hearing them in a different mode. They did not perform this live at any point and it remains part of a select group of truly obscure songs in their catalogue. Not so much a 'deep cut' as an oddball.

'Chameleon' (John Fogerty)

The third track heads to Memphis, to 926 East McLemore St, the home of Stax Records. It's not their first visit. Wilson Pickett's 'Ninety Nine and a Half' popped up on their first album and southern soul, in general, was a component of their sound from the beginning. John Fogerty's admiration for Booker T and the MGs goes supernova on *Pendulum,* but his love of the

MGs-backed *Born Under A Bad Sign* LP by Albert King is evident throughout their career. The obvious follow-up to 'I Heard It Through The Grapevine' would have been for the band to cover a Stax classic, something by Otis Redding perhaps, but, instead, John Fogerty decided to write his own soul tune.

'Chameleon' suffers from the same problem as other songs on this record. It sounds unfinished. It's not the production but more a sense that the band hasn't got to the heart of things yet. The lyrics are okay, but, again, they seem dashed off. The chameleon idea is a good one, except that the subject seems more like she is gaslighting the singer than changing colour to camouflage herself. Like 'Pagan Baby' and 'Sailor's Lament', there is no real story, only a series of images. That can work in a song, of course, but there needs to be a beginning and an ending or punchline. The whole idea of a chameleon is that they can disappear without moving. Surely that presents an opportunity for a songwriter. John Fogerty, as I have mentioned, says that he was exhausted by the time they made this record. That is particularly obvious in the lyrics, with at least one exception, as we will see.

But 'Chameleon' is among the two or three best songs on *Pendulum*. The underwhelming and, yes, flat woodwind section provided by John Fogerty and no one else is a misstep but otherwise, this song cooks and fulfils the promise of a great soul-style groover. The chord changes are engaging, and the electric piano part adds colour. Stu lays down the funk with Doug's signature rolls punctuating things. Tom's rhythm guitar, one of the features of this record, shines here too. If only someone had been able to talk John Fogerty into hiring one of the thousands of tenor sax players who would have been grateful for the work. Here's my 'hot take': More time in rehearsal, another run at the lyrics, and King Curtis on sax. Another top ten single. I simply can't understand the reluctance to use guest musicians, particularly for a traditional four-piece band. The funny thing is that they invited Booker T and the MGs, who opened shows for them at the time, to a jam session which was filmed for a television special and is available as a bootleg. Would it not have made sense to ask Booker T Jones to play keyboards on this album and to bring Wayne Jackson along for sax duties? It's possible that Fantasy wouldn't pay, I don't know, but it does seem like a missed opportunity. Nevertheless, this remains a standout track on the record.

'Have You Ever Seen The Rain?' (John Fogerty)

One of the things that can make an album disappointing is the inclusion of one, and only one, absolute classic track. That sounds counterintuitive, but if *Pendulum* was going to be their experimental album or their rough diamond, the whole project is upended by the presence of 'Have You Ever Seen The Rain?' It's a lot of people's favourite CCR song and in the context of the Creedence catalogue, it is several steps above the other material on this record. It's as though 'Sympathy For The Devil' was the fourth song on *Their Satanic*

Majesties Request. You could have strong feelings about that album either way, but those feelings would be seriously complicated if you had to reckon with one of the Stones' best songs on the same album as 'Gomper'. Yes, I realise that '2000 Light Years From Home' is on that record. Stay with me! 'Have You Ever Seen The Rain?' isn't only the best song on the album or one of the best CCR songs; it's a great single, period. And it puts the rest of the record in the shade.

Like their other rain song – has any other band scored two top ten hits with the word rain in both titles? – this one has become something of a climate change song. The rain won't stop in some places like Puerto Rico or New Orleans but doesn't happen enough in other places. John Fogerty, however, wrote it about his band. He felt that despite all their success, no one was happy, hence the rain coming down on a sunny day. Some have interpreted this song as another of his counterculture panegyrics where we have arrived in the seventies, but not much has changed. Ever since Dylan's 'Hard Rain', any mention of precipitation will be interpreted as bombs, so some, at the time, thought this was a reference to the bombs 'raining' down on, not only Vietnam but Cambodia. It doesn't seem to be that kind of song but, as with 'Who'll Stop The Rain', it is adaptable. As a listener, you can decide what's coming out of the sky.

Tom Fogerty was about to leave, but he left his mark on his final single with the band. His rhythm guitar work, along with Stu Cook's lyrical bass work, brings this song to life. John Fogerty puts down his Les Paul to play the organ on this one. It's a simple song structurally, somewhere between a folk song and a fifties ballad. The verse is two chords, but the descending pattern in the chorus provides the song with real character.

They never performed this song on stage though all the surviving members have played it live at one point or another. There is some possibility that they did it at the disastrous release party, but no one remembers. It may be the most covered of all Creedence songs, with versions by everyone from Boney M to Rod Stewart to Belinda Carlisle. A Johnny Cash version for his *Rainbow* album is promising until you hear the schmaltz production. The Ramones give it their standard treatment, but the most moving cover is by The Minutemen, CCR superfans, who recorded a heartfelt version for their final album before D. Boon's tragic death.

'(Wish I Could) Hideaway' (John Fogerty)

This is a Creedence song that deserves to be better known. Hank Bordowitz, the author of *Bad Moon Rising: The Unofficial History of Creedence Clearwater Revival* (1998), says that this is John Fogerty at his most 'vocally vulnerable.' The song is believed to be about the problems in the band and it does read like a plea to his brother, who was about to depart. 'Well, I know/You really never/Liked the way it all goes down/Go on, hideaway'. There's something poignant too about the second verse where he says, 'Think it's gonna rain/Oh, what's the difference?/Is there some way I can help?' Is this a reference to their two rain songs? It's hard to tell, but these are a moving set of lyrics that capture something universal about the imminent departure of a friend.

The band are in full Stax Records mode on this one. The organ replaces the guitar for a serious soul workout. A few critics noted that Stu Cook stretched out on this record. Perhaps he is easier to hear against the organ. In any case, he plays beautifully on this song, ably supported by Doug's drumming. It is indeed one of John's great vocals. The organ playing is serviceable but not spectacular. I won't start talking about the efficacy of hired guns again but keep in mind that Booker T Jones had been in Wally Heider's studio with the band when they began working on *Pendulum*.

The band never played it live and neither John Fogerty nor the other surviving members have ever had a shot at it on stage.

'Born To Move' (John Fogerty)

In his memoir, John Fogerty only mentions this song to note a problem with Stu's bass work during the recording process. It's a shame because it is an ambitious song featuring a guitar solo, a long organ solo, a rare bass showcase from Stu, and a serious groove. The organ solo does drift into the sincerest form of flattery for Booker T at points, but Fogerty does a good job with an instrument he had only recently begun to play. Whatever his quibbles, Stu Cook is in excellent form and the chemistry between the two is a highlight of the song.

Like 'Hideaway', it is a Creedence song that should be better known. With such a punchy chorus, it might have been polished up to a successful single, but the version we have is a good indication of what Fogerty was attempting on *Pendulum*.

A truly fun version was recorded by an Australian group called The Surprise Sisters in the mid-1970s and it is well worth hearing. Their version digs out a proto-glam element in it.

'Hey Tonight' (John Fogerty)

This was on the flipside of 'Have You Ever Seen The Rain?' and is the second best-known track on *Pendulum*. It's one of the few songs on the album that the band rehearsed before coming into the studio and it shows. Along with 'Have You Ever Seen The Rain?' and one or two others, it feels fully realised and is a glimpse of what *Pendulum* might have sounded like if the band had been in a better place.

It opens with a mesmerising picked-out riff on electric guitar before the band kicks in, with Stu and Doug creating a classic CCR bottom-end groove. Tom chugs along on rhythm guitar as John pleads for a great night out. It's a celebration of music and good times. 'Gonna get it to the rafters/watch me now' is followed by 'Jody's going to get religion/All night long'. It's not entirely clear what John Fogerty means, but my hunch has always been that the gospel element in Creedence's music and rock and roll generally is being celebrated. This is Jody's second of three appearances in John Fogerty's music. He'll finally depart for the rodeo in one of John's most famous solo songs, 'Almost Saturday Night'.

Not surprisingly, the song became a live staple, though only by the trio version of the band, of course. There is a frenetic version on the *Live In Europe* album, recorded in Germany, where the song was a number one hit. It has been covered a few times, notably by Lords of the New Church, who do it up nicely in their bubbleglam style.

'It's Just A Thought' (John Fogerty)

It occurs to me reading the sombre lyrics to this song that its author was all of 25 years old when he wrote, 'All the years are passin' by and by/Still, I don't know what makes it go'. This is another soul-influenced, somewhat downcast, song on the record. Again, it would be easy to read something of the band's inner turmoil in the lyrics but is a song about regret and, indeed, the passing of time.

It sounds like Procol Harum's 'A Whiter Shade of Pale' with the organ playing the chord changes under the vocal. Stu adds some colour on bass and Doug punctuates each section with his signature rolls. It is noted as a 'deep cut' in their catalogue, and while I don't disagree, it does seem like a song that needed more time in the oven. It's one of those songs where the jam at the end sounds like the part that needed lyrics that were never written. It is, by no means, a dud. It was never played live by the band and remains unknown to all but dedicated fans of the band.

'Molina' (John Fogerty)

Molina is the bad girl daughter of the mayor who drives recklessly – in a blue car – dates the sheriff, gets arrested, and hopes to win a lot of money so her father can retire. The lyrics sound hastily arranged and the story, if there is one, is not easy to discern. Molina is like Miss Molly or The Beach Boys' fun girl in the T-Bird. Molina is trouble!

This is another great rocker like 'Hey Tonight', this time in the Little Richard mode. Tom and John let loose on guitars while the rhythm section rumbles like a diesel truck. John's pancake-flat saxophone turns up again, but the raw fifties sound of the song makes it a better fit than the soul tunes earlier on the album. Electric piano is heard here too.

It was never played live and has not been covered much, but it is a great track and a brilliant example of the band's ability to let loose on a 1950s-style rocker. Because the last track on the album is an experimental piece, 'Molina' has a certain poignancy as the last proper CCR song on an album by the original band. There was never any need for Creedence to 'get back' since they were already there anyway, but this song does sound like the band at their most elemental.

'Rude Awakening #2' (John Fogerty)

John Fogerty's feelings about this song are clear. It was supposed to be a 'collage' in the style of The Beatles' 'Revolution Number 9' and a collaborative effort. He notes that the fingerpicking section at the beginning is beautiful, but the rest is nonsense. He's right about the fingerpicking but too harsh about the rest of the song. It is, oddly enough, a grower of sorts. The organ work is imaginative and some of the sections are gently evocative. It depends, I guess, on your patience for soundscapes or collages. The Beatles' track on the *White Album* was inspired by Karlheinz Stockhausen and other avant-garde composers. Their work had a profound influence on progressive rock bands and fellow travellers like Pink Floyd. It's not what one would expect from the band responsible for 'Proud Mary', but it's not without interest.

Other songs associated with Pendulum
'45 Revolutions Per Minute, Parts One and Two' (John Fogerty)

If 'Rude Awakening #2' was a serious tilt at the avant-garde, these two oddities are lame attempts at comedy. Joke interviews, funny sounds, with all too brief snippets of actual music, they are severely dated and dreadful.

Mardi Gras (1972)

Personnel:
Doug Clifford: drums
Stu Cook: bass
Tom Fogerty: rhythm guitar
John Fogerty: guitar, voice, harmonica, keys, saxophone
Recorded: Spring 1971 Wally Heider, San Francisco, January 1972 Fantasy Studio A
Released: April 1972
Label: Fantasy
Producer(s): John Fogerty, Doug Clifford, Stu Cook
Engineer: Russ Gary
Running Time: 28:20
Highest Chart Position: US 12, UK did not chart

Jon Landau called it the 'worst album I've ever heard from a major rock band' in his 1972 review in *Rolling Stone*. Worse than *Byrdmaniax*? Worse than *Smiley Smile*? Worse than Steve Miller's *Rock Love* or The MC5's *Back In The USA*? Just joking about the last one. Landau produced it, of course. This was also the era of Bob Dylan's *Self-Portrait*. The various Beatles' truly lousy solo efforts were still a few years away, but there is something shrill to the point of hysterical about his review. *Rolling Stone* always had mixed feelings about Creedence, and Landau can't contain his anger with the now three-piece band. He says that the album will one day be known as 'Fogerty's Revenge'.

The story about this album has always been that Fogerty, fed up with the complaining from his bandmates, allowed them to write some songs and help produce the follow-up to *Pendulum*. Tom Fogerty had walked out by this point and John was starting to recognise how dire the situation around his publishing had become at Fantasy Records. As a final 'fuck you' gesture to his bandmates, his record company, and *Rolling Stone* critics, he set up the band and Saul Zaentz for a massive fall in the form of a terrible record. It's a great story but something of a fairy tale.

I should say that I like this record. I'll acknowledge that it is their worst album, but they only made six and one of them has to be last. Usually, it is listed after their first album when they are ranked. Frankly, *Pendulum*, for all its strengths, has some serious problems too. To compare them: *Pendulum* has one great Fogerty song in 'Have You Ever Seen The Rain?' *Mardi Gras* has two in 'Sweet Hitch-Hiker' and 'Someday Never Comes'. *Pendulum* has songs where John Fogerty plays organ and, ahem, tenor saxophone instead of guitar. *Mardi Gras* is all guitars. *Pendulum* suffers from some mixing issues, *Mardi Gras* does not. *Pendulum* finishes with a sound collage, *Mardi Gras* does not. This is only to suggest that it is closer to, say, *Burrito Deluxe* than The Doors' *Other Voices*, meaning that it is seriously flawed rather than seriously terrible. Ellen Willis, in a more sober assessment, wrote in the

Rolling Stone Illustrated History of Rock and Roll, that *Mardi Gras* 'wasn't bad, only mediocre. Its rock was softened and countrified'.

The real story is of a band on the verge of breaking up. Tom's departure, John's exhaustion, and Fantasy Records' greed had taken their toll. Before *Pendulum*, John Fogerty had agreed to let the others write some songs for the album that would come after it. He stuck to his promise but in a manner that was far too abrupt. The Beatles – who John Fogerty blames for giving his guys the idea that a band could be more collaborative – slowly allowed George to grow as a songwriter. Fogerty, from early in their career, needed to encourage the others to write and to write with them. Throwing them into the deep end when the band was selling millions of records was a tactical error. Somewhere in an alternative universe, a version of this record exists with five classic Fogerty songs, a cover or two, and the best Stu and Doug songs, with John singing. It's a disappointing finish and Creedence fans deserved better.

The good news is that, despite his strategy, John Fogerty remained in charge and set out to create a Creedence album. You get two stunning originals from John, another pretty good one, and the obligatory rockabilly cover. If you are prepared to have an open mind, you get a couple of reasonable songs from Doug and Stu. The bad news is that this one has a few real truly mediocre moments. Up until *Pendulum*, Creedence did not do much that was mediocre. Those tracks might have been redeemed somewhat with John Fogerty's vocals but they take the new democratic ideal too far and everyone gets to sing. That only works if everyone can do it. The Band had more capable singers than most groups, but they never divided things evenly just for the sake of it.

So what is *Mardi Gras*? A disappointing final effort? A major misstep? A one-finger salute to Fantasy Records? All of above? What it isn't is a misunderstood masterpiece or wildly underrated gem. At its best, there is a weariness in the sound that has seeped into Creedence by this stage. Give it a chance. I'm sure that 'The Dude' would say that it's better than The Eagles.

'Lookin' For A Reason' (John Fogerty)

The album opens with the old dinosaur victrola listening to Buck Owens again. The most straightforward country song ever recorded by the band finds John Fogerty finally playing a Fender Telecaster and exploring its twangy possibilities in style. John Landau calls this 'fluff', but I disagree. *Mardi Gras*, taking the obvious problems out of the story for a second, demonstrates a definite turn away from Memphis towards that other Tennessee music hub, Nashville. More accurately, it shows the influence of the scene that had been developing at the Palomino Club in North Hollywood. What came to be known as 'country rock' is a slippery beast to net, but albums like The Byrds' *Sweetheart of the Rodeo*, The Beau Brummels' *Bradley's Barn*, Bob Dylan's *Nashville Skyline*, The Flying Burrito Brothers' *Gilded Palace of Sin*, along with Ian and Sylvia Tyson's Great Speckled Bird project and The Grateful

Dead's *Workingman's Dead* are evidence that something was in the air. The Palomino Club was a venue that hosted country acts in LA but was slowly taken over by hip young rockers in Nudie suits. Later, it was an important staging ground for 'Americana', but that is, as they say, another song.

Creedence had the chops to do country and had been dabbling in it for years. John Fogerty's first solo album, *Blue Ridge Rangers*, makes it clear where he was headed. For the record, he began to wear cowboy hats and shirts in this period. 'Lookin' For A Reason' sounds far more Bakersfield than Nashville, but by opening the album with it, the band is making a statement. Soul? That was the last album. Listen to that pedal steel!

The lyrics don't hold back. John Fogerty was going through a divorce at the time, but it is hard not to hear something about the situation with the band in lyrics like, 'Every night, I ask myself again/Just what it was that made our dream begin/It seemed like a good idea way back then/But I'm wondering now what daydream took me in'. Ouch. It was never played live. A Finnish version exists.

'Take It Like A Friend' (Stu Cook)

If you ever feel tempted to regard John Fogerty as the bad guy in the Creedence story, it is worth googling the lyrics to this Stu Cook original:

> If maybe you'd move over,
> Gave someone else a chance to try their luck,
> Instead, you run up closer,
> Trying to grab a page before they close the book.

That's only the first verse. Here's the second:

> Thought you had the honor,
> Took special pride in all your well laid plans.
> Forgot about the others,
> We moved out toward the light showing empty hands.

And John Landau thought the album was boring! So far, it is like an Italian opera. John gives his view in 'Lookin For A Reason', Stu responds. I think this is a song about John Fogerty. The irony is that he is moving over here and remembering the others. I've tried not to take sides in this book, but whatever the situation, this is a seriously unpleasant song. The final verse touches on the band's financial situation:

> Love to be the winner.
> Gather up your chips in time to cash 'em in.
> We're all looking thinner,
> Playing cards too close for either one to win.

The rumour has always been that John Fogerty did not play on this song and that Stu himself is on lead guitar here. If that's true, he's imitating Fogerty with some success.

This is not a highlight. It's a lame song with vile lyrics, badly sung and indifferently played. Stu is no singer and nothing about this song is impressive. Even the title is awful. Take it like a friend? Not likely.

'Need Someone To Hold' (Doug Clifford and Stu Cook)

Things pick up considerably on the third track on Side One. Doug Clifford proves to be a far more capable singer than his rhythm section partner. This has a whiff of The Band about it and works well as a mid-tempo country rocker. Cosmo avoids commenting on the CCR situation (I think!) with a song about loneliness co-written by Stu Cook. Again, the rumour was that John did not appear on the song, but it is likely that he had some hand in arranging it, if not actually playing guitar or singing. This song, with some assistance and vocals from John, could have been a highlight of the record. As it stands, it's a pretty good song.

'Tearin' Up The Country' (Doug Clifford)

On this one, Doug unearths the Jerry Lee Lewis circa 1968 voice that will feature on his 1972 solo record, *Cosmo*. This isn't anyone's idea of a deep cut, but it has the Bakersfield groove and is by no means unlistenable. Doug has a voice and his drummer's timing works well in his singing.

'Someday Never Comes' (John Fogerty)

This is one of John Fogerty's finest moments. A lot of songs about parenting lean towards the 'Forever Young' side of things, dreamy odes to the magic of child-rearing. There's certainly room for that sort of song, but with 'Someday Never Comes', John Fogerty makes plain a situation that would become increasingly common as the children of divorced parents began to have their own kids. And get divorced. Fogerty's own father had walked out when he was young and now, as his band and marriage fell to pieces, he found himself in the same situation. The circular nature of life and the emotional weight of one's own experiences that come into play when you have your own child are all part of this song. In the song, he juxtaposes the old parental saw, 'Someday you'll understand' with the bleak reality that the 'someday will never come.' He beats Harry Chapin to the 'Cat's In The Cradle' punch by raising the possibility that we will all become our own parents in some measure.

And it rocks. It's an angry song that opens with strummed guitar chords and an insistent beat from Doug Clifford that suggests that things will speed up. Stu's bass on the first beat of each bar builds considerable tension in the verses. When it goes into the chorus, it heads into 'Fortunate Son' territory long enough to suggest repressed rage. John Fogerty has said that he was disappointed with the recording because he thought the chorus should have sounded like '15 Marshalls on 11 in the background going rrrr'. I understand what he means, but I think he gets the effect he is seeking. For a 2013 collaborations album called *Wrote A Song For Everyone*, he rerecorded the song with LA band, Dawes. Fogerty says that it 'surpasses the Creedence track'. It's worth hearing, but I do not agree. The emotion in the original is raw and though Fogerty doesn't think so, his former bandmates are the perfect foil for this type of song.

The band never performed it live though John Fogerty has done so on occasion. It remains one of the great tearjerkers in rock and roll. A reviewer in the ultra-hip *Creem* magazine was reduced to weeping by it in 1972. It is not nearly as well known as Cat Stevens' 'Father and Son' or the Harry Chapin song but is less stagey than either. John Fogerty isn't playing around here. This is personal!

'Someday Never Comes' was the final 45 from the band and the first not to reach the Top Ten since 'I Put A Spell On You' in 1968. It reached 25 on the Billboard Charts. 'Tearin Up The Country' was on the flipside.

'What Are You Going To Do?' (Doug Clifford)
This is another Doug Clifford song and it has been interpreted as yet another one about the state of Creedence Clearwater Revival. It could as easily be a standard 'make up your mind about me' song. Doug does okay on this one. Even Jon Landau thought this was one of the better moments on the album but suggests that with John on vocals – he was the singer in the band after all – it would have been a real proposition.

The chorus hook, 'What are you gonna do? Forget about your mother and think about you' works better in the song than on paper. It has the feel of a summer song if lacking the heft of CCR's previous entrants in that category.

'Sail Away' (Stu Cook)
If *Mardi Gras* isn't the worst album by a major band, this is surely the most inept vocal performance ever to appear on a major band's album. Stu Cook is flat here and not in the standard Lou Reed way, just flat like a work colleague in a karaoke bar. 'Sail Away' isn't a bad song at all. John Fogerty could have made something of this one. It's an appealing chord progression and Stu's bass line provides a real groove.

It's difficult, particularly in the context of this album, not to read the lines, 'Spent a long time listening to the captain of the sea/Shouting orders to his crew', as one more shot over the bow, as it were.

The title of this album suggests parades and fun. They should have called it, 'Our Dysfunctional Band is About To Break Up'. That's two songs so far from Stu paying out at John Fogerty, one response from John and a possible from Doug. The recording sessions must have been a barrel of laughs. 'Hey John, here's another one I wrote about how angry I am at you'. 'Thanks, Stu, I'll just plug in my guitar so we can get started'.

'Hello Mary Lou' (Gene Pitney)

Ricky Nelson is sometimes forgotten in discussions of rockabilly. His movie-star looks and his role on the *Ozzie and Harriet* television show have overshadowed his music. With John Fogerty's ultimate hero, James Burton, on guitar, Nelson served up a whole series of top-shelf rockabilly sides in the late 50s. Songs like 'Stood Up', 'Waiting In School', and the haunting 'Lonesome Town' are part of the canon. By the early '60s, the material was softened slightly in line with the teen idol craze, but with Burton beside him, he couldn't help but make great music. 'Hello Mary Lou' from 1961, written by Gene Pitney, was his highest-charting single in the UK and arguably his most famous song. By that time, The Blue Velvets would have been covering the hits of the moment and they certainly would have played this one.

Creedence plays it straight. Fogerty drops the growl and sings like Nelson. The guitar solo is a tribute to James Burton, an important influence. Stu Cook and Doug Clifford are more than capable of laying down the rhythm for this song and, in the midst of all the animosity, one can only hope that they had some fun recording it. It's a highlight of the record.

'Door To Door' (Stu Cook)

The lyrics to this final Stu Cook original on the album are by far his best. He writes from the point of view of a door-to-door salesman using the language of the profession. Door-to-door selling is now a thing of the past, but it was once commonly practised and became an attractive option for moderately charming men without resources or training.

It was not glamourous, and Cook's song captures something of the exhaustion of the job. He doesn't sing it very well, but it's one of the better songs here.

CCR didn't record many shuffle rhythm songs. Fogerty suggests, bitterly, in his book, that Doug Clifford couldn't play them, but that can't be true. The band sounds great here and on the various live versions. This was the only non-Fogerty song to make it onto their setlists when they toured in 1972. A version can be heard on various bootlegs and on the official *Live In Europe* album. Stu Cook's vocals are better there, and it is worth hearing.

I like this song. If you put this on at a party, people would dance and ask who it was. The record company must have had some faith in it because it appeared on the B-side of 'Sweet Hitch-Hiker'. Along with that song, it was the last recording the band did at Wally Heider Studios in San Francisco.

'Sweet Hitch-Hiker' (John Fogerty)

The final track is, appropriately, their final visit to the top ten. It's a full-throttle rocker that is best heard on a crackling AM radio while driving to the beach on a hot summer day. It's doesn't have the gravity or the subtlety of some of their earlier hits but is another example of John Fogerty's knack for capturing a moment of freedom and joy in a simple song.

A promo video made at the time makes the meaning of the song clear. A guy sees a beautiful hitchhiker and thinks about picking her up. Later he is hitchhiking and she drives by, leaving him wondering what might have been. It's mildly salacious – won't you ride on my fast machine? – but innocent in the context of 1972. The film clip intersperses live footage with shots of mini-skirted beauties and the band on motorcycles. As hitchhiking songs go, this is more Beach Boys than Doors.

Doug Clifford said the vibes were great when they were recording the song at Wally Heider not long after Tom had left the band. It was their first recording as a three-piece and there must have been a sense that the band still had a future. It's heavier than their earlier singles but wouldn't have been out of place on the radio in 1972. John Fogerty is in good voice and knocks out riff after riff on his Les Paul. Any further doubts about Stu and Doug's fitness to back him should be erased by this track. Stu, in particular, lifts the whole thing with a funky bassline. If *Mardi Gras* is disappointing, it is because songs like 'Sweet Hitch Hiker', 'Someday Never Comes' and, if we are being generous ', Door To Door', suggest that there was life in the band yet. The decision to downgrade John's contributions was a misstep, but if they had found some way to resolve the squabbles and make peace with Fantasy Records, they would have been able to continue. Unfortunately, endings are messy and this one, which would eventually make it to the Supreme Court in the 1990s, was one of the messiest. *Mardi Gras* demonstrates both how bad things were in the band by 1972 and how much good music they were still capable of making.

Live Albums

Creedence Clearwater Revival did not release any live albums when the band was together, so these first two records are part of a long series of repackagings and assorted cash-ins by Fantasy. The long-awaited Woodstock set is a much more recent release and one presumably sanctioned by John Fogerty, who has made his peace with Fantasy Records. That said, they were a great live act and all of these recordings reveal a band that rocked pretty hard on stage. John Landau, in his original *Rolling Stone* review of *Live In Europe*, observed that John Fogerty was 'looser' live. A lot of artists have a different personality onstage, but Fogerty does seem to lose some of his perfectionist instincts there. That's good when things like 'Fortunate Son' and 'Sweet Hitch-Hiker' get turned into proto-punk onslaughts and not so much when 'Lodi' is dispatched in a perfunctory manner. Sadly, there are no unreleased tracks or unusual covers on any of these 'official' releases. If someone has a recording of one of their sets at Dino and Carlo's from 1967 or the Avalon in 1968, I'd love to hear it. They were likely playing all sorts of different songs and trying out originals that didn't make the albums. Unlike his contemporary, Neil Young, John Fogerty was not given to discarding songs or entire albums. There are deep cuts, but the lost masterpieces simply don't exist. Doug Clifford occasionally makes noises about music in the vaults, but nothing has ever appeared, officially or otherwise.

Live In Europe (Fantasy Records 1973)

These are recordings from a series of dates in September of 1971. Tom was long gone by this time, so this is, as John Fogerty has termed it, the three-legged stool in action. The sound quality on this double album is somewhere between fair and good, better than bootlegs, nowhere near the live albums that were appearing at the time. But then, those were usually extensively overdubbed and remixed. By the time this appeared, the band was history and John Fogerty's relations with Fantasy were not particularly cordial. This is the band as audiences in Germany, Belgium, Holland, Denmark, Sweden, and the UK heard them in September of 1971. As there are no outtakes of well-known songs like 'Proud Mary', this is an opportunity to hear the band playing the song as it has evolved over three years. I like John Fogerty's guitar sound on the live records. There was always a garage element in Creedence, but his 'plug in and turn it up' approach live makes it clear.

Highlights: The version of Stu Cook's 'Door To Door' is much better here. 'Fortunate Son' sounds like the punk anthem it was always meant to be.

The Concert (Fantasy Records 1980, originally released as The Royal Albert Hall Concert)

Remember the famous Bob Dylan 1966 Royal Albert Hall recording that turned out to have been recorded at Manchester Free Trade Hall? Well, this is the not-so-famous Royal Albert Hall live album that turned out to have been recorded in Oakland. The Dylan album was a bootleg, so no one was that worried, but this was an official release by Fantasy Records. No one was too worried about this one either by 1980, but Fantasy owned up and re-released the album as *The Concert*. Somewhere John Fogerty was shaking his head.

Their excuse: 'The tapes were in the wrong box'. Right up there with the dog ate my homework. The tip-off was the casual mention of nearby San Bernardino at the beginning of 'Tombstone Shadow'.

This is much better than *Live In Europe*. The show took place at the Oakland Alameda County Colosseum on 31 January 1970, which puts it amid the *Cosmo's Factory* recordings. 'Who'll Stop The Rain' b/w 'Travelin Band' had recently been released, so the band was at the height of its powers. John Fogerty's creative output was in overdrive. The album represents their usual setlist at the time and it is ridiculously familiar. If the album was called Greatest Hits Live, no one would quibble. The sound quality is much higher here and, what you hear is what the audience heard in 1970. There is some footage available of this show which is well worth viewing.

Highlights: 'Don't Look Now' is stunning. If the rockabilly element is restrained on the album version, it's off the leash here.

Live At Woodstock (Fantasy Records 2019)
One of the fascinating things about the Woodstock Festival in August of 1969 is that the recordings reveal how fast music was moving in the late 1960s. The stars of Monterey Pop two years earlier – Hendrix, The Who, Janis, and The Jefferson Airplane – are all back but, to be honest, seem battle weary. Before you throw the book across the room, at least acknowledge that Santana – who were not that well known yet – and Sly And The Family Stone – still a rising act – put in the two best performances on the original 3LP record. My point is that 1969 was a long way from 1967 in rock and roll time and there is a Janus-faced aspect to the festival, which makes it both a celebration of the turbulent years that preceded it and a snapshot of what was happening in rock and roll that very week.

And that week, 'Green River' was on the charts and Creedence was arguably the biggest band in the US. They were apparently the first band to sign on to play the festival. Some writers have suggested that it couldn't have happened at all without their support. Their presence reassured managers who had to figure out if it was worth the scheduling hassle during the busy summer.

They were given what, on paper, was a prime spot on the Saturday schedule. Janis Joplin was the headliner and they were on before her. Along with Janis, they would be the icing on the cake of a great day. The audience would be primed for their set by all the great acts that came first and ready to go crazy. Except that isn't what happened.

The rain delayed an already loose schedule and they ended up playing early on Sunday morning. They also followed their old nemeses, The Grateful Dead. Jerry and his pals were terrible for several hours and the audience members were only just showing vital signs by the time Creedence took the stage.

Thus, our heroes had to wake up the crowd for their own set and Janis Joplin's. If anyone was asleep at the end of 'Keep On Chooglin'' it could only be blamed on the brown acid. Their set is electrifying. It's six months before the Oakland show and, as good as they were then, there is more hunger here in their performance and the rough edges hadn't been entirely ironed out. 'Proud Mary' is pure garage punk and 'I Put A Spell On You' sounds like righteous psychobilly.

John Fogerty wasn't happy with the sound and felt that the Dead had demolished any possibility of authentic audience reaction. He didn't agree to be in the film or on the soundtrack. For up-and-comers like Johnny Winter, it was a tactical error to opt-out of the film. For Creedence, I'm not sure it made that much difference. For years, nobody seemed to remember that they had even been there. Thus, they avoided the nostalgic aspic that preserved bands like Country Joe and The Fish as part of the 'Woodstock Generation.'

Highlights: 'Bad Moon Rising'. You've heard it a million times, but this raw version is a timely reminder of its greatness. 'Keep On Chooglin'' never sounded better. Fogerty sounds righteous on 'The Night Time Is The Right Time'. It's all pretty good, really.

Other Live Recordings
Creedence Clearwater Revival was huge at about the same time that bootlegs were beginning to circulate. Live recordings of their shows were not extensively distributed compared to other acts, but their sheer popularity meant that a few were always available. These recordings can be heard online these days. This is by no means an exhaustive list but rather a taster of what is out there. Sadly, no live recordings from 1968 appear to be available.

Fillmore West March 1969
Five or six songs (including the instrumental jam known as 'Crazy Otto') with pretty good sound quality. These are some of the same songs they played later in the year at Woodstock, but this is worth hearing.

Chicago August 24 1969
A few days after Woodstock. The sound quality is poor, but it is of some historical interest.

LA Forum August 29 1970
The sound quality is not great, but it is a different setlist, so there is a live version of 'I Heard It Through The Grapevine' and a stonking 'Ooby Dooby' to sweeten the pot.

Fillmore West July 4 1971

This was the closing night of the famous venue, so it was broadcast live in San Francisco. The sound quality is only okay, but they were on fire that evening, so it is worth your while. This recording was the basis of several popular bootleg albums.

Boston Gardens July 16 1971

Historical interest only. The sound quality is poor and it is roughly the same set as the Fillmore West show above. The last show with Tom wasn't far off by this point.

Budokan, Tokyo, Japan February 29 1972

Terrible sound but convincing performances. Of interest as an early show without Tom Fogerty.

High School Reunion, El Cerrito High 1988

It's only Doug Clifford and John Fogerty, but there is footage and they sound pretty good, all things considered. They are playing songs that they played for half a million people at Woodstock and are, frankly, overpowering their former classmates somewhat. The footage is surreal. If Creedence had gone to your high school, this is what your 25-year reunion would have looked like.

Compilations, Boxes, etc

Creedence released roughly 65 songs across seven albums. There is one non-album B-side, 'Call It Pretending', on the other side of 'Porterville', but few outtakes and precious few alternate versions. You could buy a greatest hits album. There are tons. Fantasy, robbed of their golden goose when the band broke up, repackaged their material into a long series of singles collections and dubious compilations like *Creedence Country*. There is the 2001 Box Set which, with all of their albums, adds material from The Blue Velvets, The Golliwogs, a few bits and bobs like the pointless '45 Revolutions Per Minute' tracks from the *Pendulum* sessions, and the two live albums that had been released at that point. It's hard to find these days and was pricey at the time, considering that there was little that hadn't appeared on compilations earlier. The pre-Creedence material has been repackaged at least twice on its own by Fantasy. The Blue Velvets material is interesting but hardly mandatory.

If I haven't convinced you to buy all their albums, try the two *Chronicle* compilations. You will then have close to two-thirds of their recorded output. The first volume is all the singles from 'Suzie Q' to 'Someday Never Comes' with all the B-sides except for the two non-Fogerty songs that backed the final two. It's an excellent compilation that will leave you stunned at quantity of great songs they produced. The follow-up *Chronicle Two* collects another twenty that could have been hits. My hunch is that after the first volume, you will start buying their albums anyway. Except for *Mardi Gras*, they are usually readily available in your format of choice.

The Solo Years

The later careers of 1960s artists tend to dwarf their original lightning strikes in quantity, if not always ferocity. Creedence Clearwater Revival lasted four years and seven albums. John Fogerty's solo career is on the brink of its golden jubilee. He has released, depending on how you count them, twice as many albums as his band, although Tom Fogerty released a series of solo records after he left in 1971.

If you are curious, try 1973's *Excalibur*, featuring Jerry Garcia. Curiously, all four original Creedence members appear on 'Mystic Isle Avalon' from Tom's third album, *Zephyr National*, while Doug Clifford's *Cosmo* from the same period is a pleasant, if not life-changing experience with top players on board. Stu Cook has never done his own album although he did produce the sessions which yielded Roky Erikson's confusing array of first albums. Stu plays bass on a few tracks.

I have identified John Fogerty as the 'auteur' figure in the band and will focus on his solo career. There was intense drama behind many of these records in the form of endless legal battles with Saul Zaentz, Fantasy Records and, sadly, his former bandmates. This has all been covered by Hank Bordowitz in *Bad Moon Rising* and Fogerty himself in his memoir, *Fortunate Son*.

John Fogerty Solo

What follows is a sweeping and decidedly opinionated rundown of John Fogerty's post-Creedence studio albums. All songs mentioned are by John Fogerty unless shown otherwise.

Blue Ridge Rangers (Fantasy 1973)

In the swampiest 36 hours of my life, I once saw John Fogerty and Tony Joe White perform on successive evenings. Turns out the man behind 'Polk Salad Annie' and other excellent songs played a role in John's first solo record.

In 1972, as CCR was winding up their final tour, Tony Joe White was the opening act. After the show, a tradition developed whereby he and Fogerty would jam, the rule being no Creedence songs. From these jams emerged, for Fogerty, a remembered love of country and gospel, which had always been just under the surface in CCR. In his memoir, he draws a line from these jams to his first solo record, released the following year.

There is a case to be made that this album, accredited to the imaginary Blue Ridge Rangers, is an indication of a future Creedence album if they had stayed together. John had taken to wearing western shirts and cowboy hats on the final tour, and *Mardi Gras*, for all its faults, provides evidence the honky tonk had overtaken the swamp in John's musical imagination.

All Creedence's records, except *Pendulum*, featured cover versions and, in the manner of the Rolling Stones covering Robert Johnson, Slim Harpo, and Robert Wilkins as they developed their sound in the late sixties and early seventies, these songs were mission statements linked to the album's broader theme. With *Blue Ridge Rangers*, John Fogerty recorded no originals and let the covers speak for themselves. He played every instrument on the album and did all the singing. This attracted dismissive comments by reviewers, which is odd considering Stevie Wonder and Paul McCartney had taken the same approach so recently. The album is better produced than either *Pendulum* or *Mardi Gras*.

Reviewers weren't sure what to do with it at the time and it continues to have a mixed reputation. It has been slotted in with 'country rock'. Fogerty says he had no taste for 'hippie' country, presumably meaning The Byrds, The Flying Burrito Brothers and related acts. He didn't like the irony and wanted to pay tribute to the music he loved. He and Gram Parsons would have found little to disagree on there.

The selections suggest the same exquisite taste in country he had shown in rockabilly and soul while in CCR. Songs by Webb Pierce, Merle Haggard, George Jones, and Hank Locklin are treated with reverence. Today, these figures, especially Haggard and Jones, are widely understood to be geniuses. In 1973, their audiences knew it, but the word was still getting out.

This is an underrated and misunderstood record. The country covers are beautifully executed, while the gospel numbers and a long-forgotten 50s pop song frame the record as a unique and satisfying statement.

Highlights
'Somewhere Listening For My Name' (Archie Browlee)
This was originally recorded by the gospel act Five Blind Boys of Alabama for the Peacock label in 1953. If you haven't heard the original, prepare yourself for a transformative experience. Of all the covers on the album, this one best suits Fogerty's voice.

'Hearts of Stone' (Rudy Jackson, Eddie Ray)
There was a time, in the early 1950s, when rock and roll was a rumour that a brand of comfortable pop ruled the airwaves. There was Perry Como and there were groups of female singers like The Fontane Sisters. As it became clear tastes were changing in the wake of Bill Haley's smash with 'Rock Around The Clock', some of these folks had a shot at music that swung harder. The Fontane Sisters tried their luck in 1955 with 'Hearts of Stone'. It had been a chart-topping R&B hit for Otis Williams and The Charms the previous year. The sisters' version is a credible attempt at R&B with a cool sax solo. John Fogerty takes it into stripped-down rockabilly territory.

Two singles appeared after the Blue Ridge Rangers album with songs that would almost completely disappear from the Fogerty story. None have ever been reissued on compilation albums. All four songs are Fogerty originals, his first as a solo artist.

'You Don't Owe Me'/'Back in the Hills' (Fantasy Records 1974)
These are the final recordings credited to the Blue Ridge Rangers. They are both gems. 'You Don't Owe Me' is a killer rockabilly song that should have been a smash hit. 'Back In The Hills', interpreted as being about his withdrawal from CCR and stardom, is not miles away from the sort of jam Fleetwood Mac would soon turn into gold. Fogerty does it better.

'Coming Down The Road'/'Ricochet' (Fantasy Records 1974)
Coming Down The Road was the first single he released in his own name. The song is a serviceable, if predictable, rocker halfway between 'It Came Out Of The Sky' and the soon-to-be-released Rockin All Over The World. The flipside is an instrumental in the Booker T and The MGs mode.

John Fogerty (Asylum/Fantasy Records 1975)
This album was a revelation when I first came across it after wearing out my Creedence records in the mid-80s. *Centerfield* hadn't appeared and I was not aware Fogerty had ever recorded a solo album, let alone two. When I put it on, I was astounded by the first track on side one. 'Rockin' All Over The World'! It's Creedence!

If you haven't heard this album, you will be surprised too. It's not on par with *Green River* or *Cosmo's Factory*, but it's better than *Pendulum*. Fogerty is embarrassed about his creased jeans on the cover and says the record is not his best work. He was drifting at the time and becoming increasingly disenchanted with the music business. These memories colour his take on the album.

He acknowledges 'Rockin' All Over The World', a hit for Status Quo a few years later, and 'Almost Saturday Night', covered marvellously by Dave Edmunds, as 'flashes of brilliance in the middle of the incompetence.' Those are the standouts, but the old jazz number 'You Rascal You' and Frankie Ford's 'Sea Cruise' cook too, along with originals 'Where The River Flows' and 'The Wall', a swamp choogle.

The album was recorded at Wally Heider's studio in San Francisco, where CCR had made so much magic. Fogerty played all the instruments on the album. Listening to it on vinyl these days, I do hear the need for a good overhaul of the mix. Otherwise, it holds up.

Highlights
'Travelin' High'
A lively nod to the Southern Soul sound that helped to shape Creedence's music. This glorious upbeat song starts off like Sam and Dave's 'Hold On I'm Coming' before establishing its own horn-driven groove.

'Dream/Song'
In his memoir, he says this doesn't seem finished. I'm not sure what he means. This is one of his lovely gospel-inflected acoustic ballads and a song that should be better known.

Hoodoo (Unreleased, 1976)
John Fogerty was truly struggling by 1976. His self-titled album hadn't sold much and now he had Joe Smith from Asylum Records on the phone. 'John, this is not a good record.' It was a week before the release date. If this reads like a minor blip, remember that seven years earlier, this guy's singles were outselling The Beatles.

Sadly, Smith was right. A single called 'You Got The Magic' appeared. If you ever wanted to hear John Fogerty in disco mode, here it is. The cringeworthy chorus alone sinks this one. The album is a mixed but not fully inflated bag. There are a few undistinguished rockers here and there, one killer rockabilly cover in Jimmy Dee's 'Henrietta' and an original called 'Hoodoo Man', a Little Richard screamer in the 'Travelin' Band' mode. The final song, 'On The Run' is worth hearing too. The verses, at least, have the Fogerty magic. The whole album can be found online and Fogerty is clear Joe Smith made the right call. He is embarrassed about his disco entry and feels nothing worked on the rest of the record. He didn't make another album for ten years.

Centerfield (Warner Bros., 1985)

This album appeared in 1985 as the oldest baby boomers closed in on their dreaded 40th birthdays. I was 19 and I'd already had a gutful of that generation. From the draft dodger teachers who berated us for not wanting to change the world to the rock critics who made it clear we were late for the party, I was tired of it. By this point, too, Dylan had become a strident born-again Christian, Neil Young said nice things about Reagan, and the Starship formerly known as Jefferson Airplane was inflicting 'We Built This City' on me every morning on my radio as I got up for work. I remained a passionate Creedence fan and was sincerely happy for John Fogerty when *Centerfield* was a hit. To be honest, though, the nostalgic aspects grated on me. 'I Saw It On TV', in particular. The Kennedy assassination, The Beatles arrival in the US, Vietnam – okay, we get it! The sixties were the most important decade ever. I was trying to have my own summer of love, a personal age of Aquarius! And it wasn't easy in the mid-eighties!

I am way past forty now and the crack cocaine of nostalgia is far more tempting. Mine, John Fogerty's, anyone's! Bring back the fun! I still have reservations about this album, but it's sounding better all the time.

The title track is now in the Baseball Hall of Fame and as ubiquitous at baseball games as the seventh-inning stretch. The electronic handclaps drive me nuts, but there is something irresistible about the 'La Bamba'-style guitar intro and the emotive minor chord in the verses. CCR's more upbeat songs always evoked summer and 'Centerfield' is a shimmering Saturday morning in July.

It isn't all corndogs and line drives out past second, however. It gets very dark indeed on the song that began as 'Zanz Kant Danz' and quickly changed to 'Vanz Kant Danz' when the lawyers got involved. Saul Zaentz could dance apparently and was not having it. To up the ante, he sued Fogerty for plagiarism with 'The Old Man Down The Road'. Saul said Fogerty had shamelessly poached it from an old song called 'Run Through The Jungle'. As I explained in the *Cosmo's Factory* section, the right to compose in the Swamp Rock style is now enshrined in US law. Whatever one says about *Centerfield*, a lot of lawyers' kids got through university without the burden of student loans because of this record.

This album was recorded at The Record Plant in Sausalito and Fogerty played all the instruments.

Highlights
'Big Train From Memphis'
As must now be clear, I like hearing this man play rockabilly music. Yes, the lyrics are nostalgic, but it is a pure expression of this form bathed in echo and love.

'Mr Greed'
Another song about his favourite movie producer, presumably. It's more kickass than the other stuff on this record. This is Fogerty pissed off and rocking out.

Eye Of The Zombie (Warner Bros., 1986)

John Fogerty wasn't the only one to sink an album under its own production in this period. I understand it is now the done thing to admire Bob Dylan's 1985 album *Empire Burlesque*. It sounds as ghastly to me as it did at the time. We are now hearing alternate versions of the songs that indeed make it clear the production was the problem. A similar argument could be mounted for *Eye of the Zombie*. There is no question this record includes awkward moments lyrically but the songs, good or otherwise, are difficult to absorb through the 80s-style cocaine console production.

At the time, it must have made sense to start using other musicians on his records. In retrospect, not so much. I am a great believer in the bass guitar. If used properly, this instrument will define a song or an album or a career. The bass player on this one, Neil Stubenhaus, was part of Quincy Jones' stable and a skilled player. But he's the wrong guy for John Fogerty. The lines are too slick, too technical, and way too bland. It doesn't help that his bass is bathed in 80s glossy muck. Fogerty needs a far more idiosyncratic player. Another Jones' associate and studio maven, John Robinson, drummed on it. The percussion sounds awful on this record and that isn't Robinson's fault. Like Stubenhaus, he is a top musician with nothing to apologize for here. He isn't right for this record. Anyone who maintains that Stu Cook and Doug Clifford weren't up to the job in CCR is sentenced to *Eye of the Zombie* on headphones for eternity.

The album descends into a series of seriously misguided attempts at the sort of crass 80s 'funk' that paved the way for grunge. 'Soda Pop', in particular, makes the disco song from *Hoodoo* sound pretty good, and that's saying something. The synths that undermined *Centerfield* at points are all over this one. 'Knockin' At Your Door' is awful. I refuse to believe it is Fogerty playing guitar on this sub-Winwood mess.

I hadn't listened to this album since I only barely lasted through side one after buying it in 1986. I wanted it to be better than I remembered. It isn't. For Fogerty, it was a disaster. It halted the comeback momentum of *Centerfield* and put him right back where he had been when *Hoodoo* was rejected. It would be another 11 years before he would release another album.

Highlights
'Change In The Weather'
This has a Robert Cray vibe and stands out on the album. If only he'd gone further down this path. He improved on it much later and occasionally plays it live these days.

'Sail Away'
This is his 'Dark Eyes' moment, a gentle gem to end a wildly uneven album. Dylan fans will howl in pain at the suggestion this ballad, with its soft reggae groove, is the equivalent to the *Empire Burlesque* finisher. John Fogerty can't help it. Even on a lousy album, there is 'that song'. This is it.

Blue Moon Swamp (Warner Bros 1997)

It took John Fogerty a while to make this one. A scan of who played on the record reveals why he made three albums on his own. In his memoir, he says he went through 30 drummers. After *Eye of the Zombie*, he knew this had to be good and if he had a different bass player or three on each of the songs, so be it!

There is no question *Blue Moon Swamp* was a return to form. He turned 50 as he was finishing it, and his legal troubles were resolved, to a point. He sounds more at peace, but that's not always a good thing. The production is sharp and his guitar playing is superb from start to finish. It is, however, missing the righteous fury that could push his songs over the edge. 'Walking In A Hurricane' doesn't sound angry enough; more like a stroll in the rain. Okay, let the poor guy make an album without going through hell for once.

The songs find him back in the south, but it is a slightly different one this time. He had been spending time in Mississippi and was coming to terms with its music. This is not to say this is his blues album, only that it is informed by a new level of engagement with the legacy of the music. 'A Hundred and Ten In The Shade' levels his debt to pre-war blues with his new favourite instrument, the dobro, and a sleepy pace. 'Rattlesnake Highway' with its quasi-spoken lyrics, has a Texas blues groove. 'Bring It Down To Jelly Roll' sees him trialling Little Feat style funk.

This was the beginning of a real comeback for Fogerty, both personally and professionally. *Blue Moon Swamp* is a grower that works best late at night in the backyard after the kids have gone to bed and another bottle is opened.

Highlights
'Southern Streamline'
The album begins in style with this honky-tonking train song.

'Blue Moon Nights'
Another classic rockabilly choogle from a true master. It could be a lost Roy Orbison Sun single. Perfect.

Déjà vu All Over Again (Dreamworks 2004)

I saw John Fogerty after this one was released and was knocked out by the title song. He played Creedence songs, along with the obvious hits from his solo career. This was the only one where I didn't drive my friends insane by singing all the words with John. I'd never heard it. The idea came from the Iraq War and the fact he was witnessing history repeating itself. In 2003, I had, along with 100,000 others, marched against Australia's involvement in the 'coalition of the willing.' 12 or so years earlier, I'd marched in London against the first Gulf War. Deja Vu again, indeed. It's a haunting song. Despite the title, it isn't an artist reheating old licks. This one found John Fogerty where he was in 2004 and it remains a highlight of his solo career.

As a hundred critics have already noted, the rest of the record comes up short. It's not terrible by any stretch, just uninspiring. Mark Knopfler can't save a tired song complaining about those damn kids and their headphones called 'Nobody Here Anymore'. The Ramones attempt, 'She's Got Baggage' is unnecessary. Gentle tunes 'Honey Do', 'I Will Walk With You' and 'Rhubarb Pie' are closer to the mark. 'Old Wicked Witch' sounds like a tribute to his pal, Tony Joe White. He goes for a heavier groove on 'In The Garden' with some success.

Highlight
'Déjà vu All Over Again'
Possibly his best post-Creedence song.

Revival (Fantasy 2007)
It's not entirely clear what Fogerty was up to with this one. All his solo work addresses the legacy of CCR to an extent. Rock and roll artists must reckon with their earlier successes. There are those content to repeat themselves if the tours keep coming. Others, and Robert Plant is a good example, are fearlessly forward-looking. It's difficult. Sticking too close to the formula is a recipe for mediocrity; straying too far causes confusion and disappointment.

Fogerty, at this point, had been playing Creedence songs again in his shows for years. He was keenly aware of the difference between the reaction to Proud Mary compared to his latest single. What does one do with that information? *Revival* is not an attempt to 'revive' Creedence but a reckoning with his former band and his status as an icon of the 1960s. 'Creedence Song' is only one example. 'Summer of Love' offers up a Cream/Hendrix pastiche and nostalgia for a summer he missed entirely because he was in the army. Again, I'm not sure what he is getting at here.

The album rocks harder than the previous two records and on 'Natural Thing', he does seem to achieve a balance between nostalgia for CCR and what he wants to do now. 'It Aint Right' is a cool rockabilly tune. 'I Can't Take It No More' is another and better punk-influenced song following on from 'She's Got Baggage'.

Whatever one's opinion of this record, it is, to date, the last proper album of new songs he has released. From here on in, Fogerty will deal with his legacy more or less directly.

Highlights
'Don't You Wish It Were True'
A loping country tune with real life in it. He 'revived' this recently for the *Fogerty's Factory* album.

'Long Dark Night'
An anti-Bush administration choogle with added cool harmonica work. It's the best song on the album by miles.

The Blue Ridge Rangers Rides Again (Fortunate Son/Verve 2009)

No, that isn't a typo. It's an in-joke for those aware the first *Blue Ridge Rangers* album was a solo effort. On this follow-up, decades later, he employs a top band and heavy friends.

The concept is the same. It's mostly country covers ranging from Ray Price's 'I'll Be There', which he nails, to The Kendalls' 1977 hit, 'Heaven's Just A Sin Away'. The choices are as tasteful as they were in 1973. John Denver's 'Back Home Again', seems like an odd pick, but Fogerty manages to tame the cheese and turn it into a pretty good song. Elsewhere, there is a rocking duet with his friend Bruce Springsteen on the Everlys' 'When Will I Be Loved' and a moving version of John Prine's eco nightmare, 'Paradise'.

The only original is 'Change In The Weather', the best song by lengths on *Eye of the Zombie*. With a much more responsive band behind him, this comes together nicely. Buddy Miller's guitar work gives it far more depth and atmosphere than the earlier version. I will note other highlights, but this is worth hearing.

This album, overall, is one of his more successful releases. With Miller and Greg Leisz helping on the stringed instruments, it is a far more focused effort. T-Bone Burnett was involved in the choice of songs. This is the sort of A-team Fogerty needs to assemble someday for an album of originals. If the concept of a follow-up to a little-known early solo effort doesn't sound promising, give this one a spin. You'll be surprised.

Highlights
'Moody River' (Chase Webster)

Fogerty breathes new life into this old warhorse. Pat Boone's 1961 version is better known than the original by its author, Chase Webster. Others will recall Frank Sinatra's 1968 version from the album *Cycles*, where he appears to be suffering from a migraine on the cover. Fogerty loses Boone's annoying piano and background singers to reveal the darkness implied in the lyrics. It's an admirable salvage effort, and he is ably abetted by Buddy Miller.

'Garden Party' (Rick Nelson)

This is a poignant cover. Nelson's early rockabilly sides were an important influence on Creedence and his 'Hello Mary Lou' was a highlight on the generally poor *Mardi Gras* album. In 1972, as CCR was breaking up, Rick had a hit with this bittersweet reflection on the price of early success. The song, which describes a 50s music revival show, ends with the memorable line, 'if memories were all I sang/I'd rather drive a truck."

By 2009 when *Rides Again* was released, John Fogerty was surely all too aware of what it meant to try to put across new material to a crowd shouting for 'Bad Moon Rising'. He plays it straight as a tribute to an early hero and to underline the point. There are a couple of Eagles on here for some reason.

Wrote A Song For Everyone (Vanguard 2013)

I get the idea. A bunch of popular acts jam with John on his best-known songs. It's a celebration of his work and a tribute to an important songwriter. Okay, but none of the collaborations adds much to these songs, and I'd rather hear the originals, thanks.

Part of the problem, for me anyway, is I don't much like The Foo Fighters, Brad Paisley, Bob Seger, or Kid Rock. A lot of people do, and maybe they hear what I don't. I do enjoy My Morning Jacket's music. Their version of 'Long As I Can See The Light' doesn't grab me. I'm not the target audience. I accept that I guess.

As with its far superior predecessor, *Rides Again*, it's produced with care. The production credits suggest the various acts took an active role, so it is a rare opportunity to hear Fogerty when someone different is turning the dials. I'm trying to be positive. Some songs work better than others. Fogerty is obviously taken with Miranda Lambert and Tom Morello's run at the title track, 'Wrote A Song For Everyone'. He talks about it at length in his memoir. It's certainly the best collaboration.

Morello, as witnessed on stage with Bruce Springsteen, is a thoughtful interpreter of other people's songs and a fascinating guitarist. Miranda Lambert has the right voice for the song and she and Fogerty sound good together. Still, I'm reaching for a CCR album as I write.

Highlight
'Mystic Highway'

There are two new originals on the record, and this one is a cracker. He's headed in a more country direction with the old Fogerty magic and drama intact. Promising stuff.

Fogerty's Factory (Warner 2020)

I sure prefer this one to *Wrote A Song For Everyone*. It's appealingly ragged and full of heart. John Fogerty was one of those generous musicians whose spontaneous lockdown YouTube videos made life bearable for the rest of us. We were all at home with our kids and it was reassuring to see John Fogerty playing music with his in the backyard. If you haven't watched the 'Who'll Stop The Rain' clip where he tells the story of CCR's performance at Woodstock, it's time to do so. Unless you're a Deadhead, then maybe not.

This collects the performances. Several were recorded by John's wife Julie on her iPhone, so the production values are not high. It makes no difference. There is a warmth and vitality to them that no amount of studio finesse could reproduce.

It was a difficult and, at times, frightening period. One salvation was the opportunity to slow down and spend time with the family. This album says a lot about John Fogerty. As Auden wrote of WB Yeats, 'You were silly like us; your gift survived it all.'

Highlights
'Centerfield'
No electronic handclaps! I can love this song now.

'Blue Moon Nights'
One of his post-CCR classics in acoustic mode.

Resources
Inside Creedence by John Hallowell (Bantam 1971)
This is sometimes noted as the worst book ever written about a rock and roll band. It isn't, believe me, but it is very much of its time. It is the only book written about the band while they were together. If you can wade through a lot of near-incomprehensible sentences, there are some tantalising glimpses of the band at their peak. It has been out of print for decades but is available second-hand if you are interested.

Bad Moon Rising: The Unofficial History of Creedence Clearwater Revival by Hank Bordowitz, (Schirmer 1998)
This is a well-researched rundown of the band's career and the legal battles that followed.

Finding Fogerty: Interdisciplinary Readings of John Fogerty and Creedence Clearwater Revival by Thomas Kitts, ed. (Lexington 2012)
This is a collection of essays which occasionally drifts into the sort of academic flim-flam that says a little with a lot. The various writers, however, are big fans, and it is, generally, a compelling study of Fogerty lyrics and the Creedence phenomenon. Editor and superfan, Thomas M. Kitts has also written a biography of John Fogerty called *John Fogerty: American Son* (Routledge 2016).

Fortunate Son By John Fogerty (with Jimmy McDonough) (Black Bay 2015)
John Fogerty wrote this memoir with the assistance of the legendary Jimmy McDonogh (*Shakey, Soul Survivor*). It is strikingly honest and filled with fascinating details about the way in which his most famous songs were written and recorded. If you are tempted to read another book on Creedence, I'd start here.

The San Francisco East Bay Scene: Garage Bands From the 60's Then and Now by Bruce Tahsler (Bill Quarry 2007). This is not a book about Creedence but provides a context for the early years of the band

The 'Electric Bayou' website is a great resource and includes detailed information on John Fogerty's solo career too.

A List to Finish

A playlist of their greatest songs is too obvious, so I'll leave you with some of my favourites among their lesser-known tracks:

1. Walk on Water (*Creedence Clearwater Revival)*
2. Graveyard Train (*Bayou Country*)
3. Cross Tie Walker (*Green River*)
4. The Night Time Is The Right Time (*Green River*) Nappy Brown cover.
5. It Came Out of the Sky (*Willie And The Poor Boys*)
6. Effigy (*Willie And The Poor Boys*)
7. Ramble Tamble (*Cosmo's Factory*)
8. Chameleon (*Pendulum*)
9. Born To Move (*Pendulum*)
10. Someday Never Comes (*Mardi Gras*)

Would you like to write for Sonicbond Publishing?
We are mainly a music publisher, but we also occasionally
publish in other genres including film and television. At Sonicbond
Publishing we are always on the look-out for authors, particularly for
our two main series, On Track and Decades.

Mixing fact with in depth analysis, the On Track series examines
the entire recorded work of a particular musical artist or group. All
genres are considered from easy listening and jazz to 60s soul to 90s
pop, via rock and metal.

The Decades series singles out a particular decade in an artist or
group's history and focuses on that decade in more detail than may
be allowed in the On Track series.

While professional writing experience would, of course, be
an advantage, the most important qualification is to have real
enthusiasm and knowledge of your subject. First-time authors are
welcomed, but the ability to write well in English is essential.

Sonicbond Publishing has distribution throughout Europe and
North America, and all our books are also published in E-book form.
Authors will be paid a royalty based on sales of their book.
Further details about our books are available from
www.sonicbondpublishing.com. To contact us, complete the
contact form there or email info@sonicbondpublishing.co.uk